How To Talk Money With Kids

*The Essential Guide to Your Child's Financial
Freedom, Success and Power*

Leanda Kayess DipFP

For Helen,

my inspiration.

Foreword

Mae West, the American singer, actress and playwright famously once said, "I've been rich and I've been poor. Believe me, rich is better." She's got a point. Our habits around health, relationships and money are largely a reflection of what we learnt about the world as children. For many of us, however, the first we focus on our finances is years after we have already established deep-seated poor financial habits that create unnecessary strain on every aspect of our lives.

Money isn't everything – this is true and all the studies that explore the relationship between life satisfaction and money suggest that once you have an income that can provide you with a home, financial security and some discretionary money, additional dollars do not result in additional happiness. The task, it would seem, is to reach that baseline.

That is exactly what Leanda's book has been written to do. Based on sound neuroscientific principles and insights, it helps parents create a learning lab for their children to form solid, healthy money habits that will enable them to achieve and maintain a financial baseline later in life.

It's an important piece of work and a wonderful gift to a generation of children who will thank her for it twenty years down the track.

I commend it to you.

Peter Burow
CEO
NeuroPower

"*How to Talk Money with Kids* is a great read if you are passionate about the children in your life and their ultimate financial success and, if living a life of abundance is one of your passions, then this book is for you!"

Janet Bray Attwood
Co/author NY Times Bestseller,
The Passion Test

Acknowledgements

Although I have studied human behavior throughout my working life, I owe a lot of my recent knowledge in this area to Peter Burow and the book of his lifework – 'NeuroPower - An exploration of human personality, integration, consciousness and nobility through the application of the four maxims of NeuroPower', and to Shelley Evans-Wild who has worked with Peter to bring his book to life through her amazing talent to apply and teach frameworks of the human system.(1) Peter's work is the most elegant and complete framework of the human system I have seen to date, and I thank Peter, Shelley and their teams for bringing it to the world.

Over the years in Financial Planning, I have sought to simplify the concepts of money to pass on the basic lessons to as many people as possible. Two teachers I thank and draw heavily on are Robert Kiyosaki and Sharon Lechter. Whilst I don't agree with everything in Robert's books, his 'Rich Dad Poor Dad' series with Sharon's input on accounting concepts, presents the seemingly daunting subject of money in some very simple to understand ways. I have used their frameworks in my financial planning and coaching work to great effect, and represent relevant key learning points in this book.

My third source of inspiration and learning is Greg Smith, author, and developer of 'Kids Money'. Greg has written seventeen books on the subject of money, including three for children, and one as a guide for parents.

I have had much encouragement as I've started on my writing path. My dear friend Helen Bairstow got me going. She was the one who insisted I help more people by sharing what I've learned about overcoming our money biases and managing money better.

Janet Bray-Attwood and Peter Burow kindly contributed the forewords. Friends and family have proof-read my work and offered great suggestions to make it more accessible.

Thanks from the bottom of my heart to each of you whether specifically named here or not. You're help and encouragement means so much to me.

CONTENTS

"It is not what you do for your children, but what you teach them to do for themselves, that will make them successful human beings." Ann Landers

ATTENTION all parents of young (and not so young) children

Why Read This Book?

Every parent I have ever met has expressed in some way or another, the same sentiment when it comes to our children. We all want our children to have a better life than us. This is especially true of their handling of money, as we've all had our share of financial blunders (some more than others), and we certainly don't want to pass our less than useful money habits onto our children. Does this sound like you? If so, I'd like nothing more than to help you.

It might not look it on first glance, but this book is all about sustainability. Teaching our children to effectively manage the main means we use to live our lives (i.e. Money) is, I argue, one of the most precious gifts we can give this and future generations.

Think about it – what is the cause of most conflict in our lives?

Arguments over money can spoil our personal relationships, our commercial relationships, and relationships within and between nations. We all have a role to play in better managing these conflicts where we encounter them, and providing our children with a more mindful and equitable system for handling money.

Let me explain who I am. My name is Leanda Kayess. I have a background in Financial Services- 30 years, 11 of these advising clients as a Financial Planner. A keen student of human behavior, more recently I have developed an interest in the advancements neuroscience has added to our understanding of this science. In my books, and via my website www.kidsmoneyrules.com, I bring to you what I have learned and applied throughout my career.

As a Financial Planner I saw the results of good money management in the clients I served– clients who had learned how to manage their money well, and were self-sufficient, generous people in retirement. These clients came from many different financial circumstances – high income earners to low income earners, people who had inherited and kept their wealth to people who had built their wealth from nothing, some who had led a blessed life to those who had encountered hardship. I'm proud to say that I practiced what I preached with my own family's finances and was able to change course without major financial upset when our one and only child came to us by surprise in 2005.

I've also been acutely aware of those I was unable to help due to the commercial reality of running a Financial Planning practice. The well meaning, hard working people who for one reason or another had missed the lesson of how to keep enough of their money to sustain themselves throughout their whole lifetime. If this is you, this book is for you and anyone you know who wants to break the cycle of scarcity of money in their family's life and the constant stresses that result from a feeling of never having 'enough'.

For many, the very mention of the word 'money' incites a deep seated fear. The fear of going into uncharted waters, the fear of putting our guard down, and ultimately, the fear that we will fail our children. There's an unspoken 'taboo' when it comes to the subject of money. A 'taboo' I aim to dispel here and now.

I come at this subject from 2 main viewpoints.

1. I believe we are each doing the best we can with the resources we've got – these resources include our money as well as our current knowledge, values, beliefs, attitudes and skills. Many of you reading this may have felt some fear, resentment or embarrassment around money – there is no need for this if you are willing to tap into some new resources and learn a better way.

2. I believe this earth has more than enough money to go around, if we can each play our part in managing it. The starting point is in managing our own money. In fact, the starting point is even more basic than that – it is in learning to manage ourselves and the way in which we each fulfil our needs.

This is the basis of my books – that we can learn to consider each of our main needs in life and allocate sufficient of our money to satisfy each one of them. These needs may not be what you think. Certainly, food, water and shelter are basic to our survival, but what we need for a truly significant and sustainable life is much more comprehensive.

As human beings, we have 6 main needs that, if satisfied in a healthy way, provide the basis of a great life. These needs play out every moment of every day in our thoughts, our feelings and our actions. If not healthy, the impetus to satisfy these needs can play havoc in our lives, and rob us of the opportunity to live the rich, abundant life we each truly deserve.

In this book, I set out what each of these needs are, how they play out in our lives, and for those who are interested, the cool ways they are showing up in neuroscience. I argue that we need to allocate money to the satisfaction of each of these needs and teach our children to do the same.

You may be thinking "but I don't have enough income", or "but I have too much debt" – I challenge you to read on regardless. I've seen many of my clients succeed despite significant financial hurdles. Often, satisfaction of our true needs does not have to involve large financial outlay.

1. Pocket Money or Allowance?

This book is written for an international audience, so I've used the word 'allowance' throughout meaning money paid to children by their parents or guardians. In some countries, the words 'pocket money' are used to denote the same thing. Also, 'pocket money' is often used in reference to younger children, and 'allowance' is used once children have learned to manage their money and are required to pay for some of their own living expenses.

2. Currency

I've used the words dollars and cents throughout this book, but please read it with your own currency in mind.

3. Roles

I see my role as being your guide to a less stressful life through better understanding and management of money. This book is the handbook for you to learn for yourself, with new ideas, practical exercises and activities you can use to help your children get these valuable lessons – the younger the better!

And I see your role as being a steward of money for your family, your community, and the wider world we live in. You are also the one your children look up to for guidance in all matters of life, including money. As parents and caregivers, the greatest gift we can give is to pass our learning onto our children. One day, they will thank you!

"It is the logic of consumerism that undermines the values of loyalty and permanence and promotes a different set of values that is destructive of family life." Christopher Lasch

Part 1 - What's Gone Wrong?

Our grandparents and great-grandparents led lives with many stresses including the great depression, 2 world wars, and the fight for women's rights which changed the way family income is generated. Money was tight, and caused stress at times, but not the constant underlying stresses we see today. In the main, people lived within their means and saved any surplus towards larger purchases. Banks lent only if their customer had savings, and could easily afford the repayments. Affordability of repayments was based on one wage, not two.

Some say our current young adults and parents have missed the boat when it comes to money. There is much evidence to support this assertion, and I have presented some of the evidence sourced from the internet and the press in Appendix A. Record levels of personal debt and children remaining a financial burden for their parents for longer are 2 major pressures that are combining to make your job as a parent more difficult.

There Are Many Places to Lay Blame

Here are 3 key societal trends we can blame:

1. Work Practices

Work practices throughout the world are watering down job security by taking positions that have traditionally been permanent and making them temporary or casual. In Australia, the Australian Council of Trade Unions (ACTU) commissioned a study chaired by former Deputy Prime Minister Brian Howe entitled 'Inquiry into Insecure Work'. Mr Howe stated in a media release on 20/3/2012 that "while the growth of insecure work mirrored global trends, the development had been more pronounced in Australia."

"It is difficult for workers in insecure employment to plan their future or be confident they will even have a job into the future," he said. "Many of these jobs deny workers the reliable income, permanency, security, and conditions and entitlements that permanent jobs offer."

2. Commercialisation of Children

Marketing is so much more prominent in society and messages are targeted at younger and younger audiences. This has created the "I" generation - coined by the Australian Bureau of Statistics after the 2006 Census to mean those with access from age 0 to the internet, but recast by Greg Smith from Kids Money as the following:

> "*This is the "I" generation, the "instant" generation, a generation of children who have never had to wait for anything...well not for long anyway!!! They have to have the new iPod NOW!! They have to have the latest phone YESTERDAY!!...*"

Commercialisation of children is a deliberate marketing strategy by companies today. Consider the promo for the YouTube video 'Consuming Children – The Commercialization of Children':

> "*With virtually no government or public outcry, the multi-billion dollar youth marketing industry has been able to use the latest advances in psychology, anthropology, and neuroscience to transform American children into one of the most powerful and profitable consumer demographics in the world. American children now influence an estimated $700 billion in annual spending, targeted virtually from birth with a relentless bombardment of sophisticated commercial appeals designed to sell everything from Hollywood*

merchandise and junk foods to iPods, cell phones, the family car and vacations. The result is that childhood itself has been commercialized. Drawing on the insights of experts, industry insiders, and children themselves, Consuming Children traces the evolution and impact of this disturbing and unprecedented phenomenon, exposing the youth marketing industry's controversial tactics and exploring the effect of hyper-consumerism on the actual lived experience of children."

3. Cashless Society

The way we handle money today has implications we are only just beginning to understand. The move to a cashless society began in Australia in the mid 1980's when credit cards changed the way we could shop. From a very tentative start, viewed with much suspicion by householders then, the way we transact much of our commercial lives has changed radically.

Most of our transactions now are cashless – we don't actually handle the hard currency anymore.

Consider a typical shopping expedition these days. Mom takes the children to the supermarket. They take the trolley through the checkout. Mom hands over her credit card, gets cash out, and wheels away the trolley full of groceries. Think about it from the child's point of view – you go to the shops, you get food and other cool stuff, **and** you get money. Mom may have explained that she is actually using her own money because it is in the bank, but even if the children see the money going in (*and who deposits cash these days?*), how the family gets money and outlays money is just an abstract concept.

How to Improve our Own, and our Children's Money Skills

The good news is that our behavior **can** change – by choice or by necessity. We are already seeing evidence of this around money in increased savings and debt repayment rates across developed nations in response to the Global Financial Crisis.

In this book I bring in insights we can draw from Psychology, Social Networking, and the rapidly evolving study of the brain via Neuroscience.

One of the keys to working well with money is to recognise that most of us have some sort of emotional charge attached to money, and that this is just our stuff. Money itself just is – it has no emotions. Working with money is best done when we are using our rational brain. This is easier said than done. Most of our waking hours are spent running on 'autopilot'. This autopilot state is not rational. It is the collection of habitual responses we have taken onboard throughout our lives to allow us to survive in a world full of things vying for our attention. At the time we first took on a habitual response, there was emotion involved. Any time we are called on to examine and change a habitual response, there will be emotion involved. In this book, I challenge you to notice your emotional responses to money, and to rise above these to look rationally and mindfully at your own habitual patterns with money.

Early childhood development studies by noted psychologists explain that as children we take on 'scripting' which forms a strong narrative throughout life. In other words, what we learn in early childhood becomes a large part of the 'story of our life'. As such, it is difficult to change the longer we have it and live by it. However, it can be changed, and even better, we can equip our children with healthier 'scripts' if we are more mindful ourselves of what and how they are learning. Most of our learning is done more by observation and imitation than by taking on board what we are told, and this points to a need to teach by example and from an early age the lessons of responsibility for self and money.

Are you mindful of what your children are learning about money?

Whether or not you mindfully teach them, children will pick up at random the habits and behaviors of their primary caregivers, whether useful or not.

Furthermore, children want to learn about money and instinctively look to their parents for this knowledge.

Social networking is fast becoming a huge influence on children. The networks they choose to belong to online will also contribute to the knowledge and behaviors children learn about money as they grow into their teens and beyond.

The 2011 findings of the MoneySense Research Panel in the UK give us some insight into some of the scripting children are picking up:

- *"English teens expect to earn most (£57,000), compared to those in Northern Ireland who anticipate earning £39,000. Both are significantly above the actual rate of £24,000.*
- *9 in 10 children think it's important to learn about money, and are more concerned about debt than any other year since 2007.*
- *71% of young people would like their parents to teach them about finance.*

This strongly contrasts with adult's opinions:

- *The majority of adults believe teens will be earning £25k at the age of 35.*
- *Nearly 80% of parents don't consider money a top priority to discuss with their children.*
- *Despite teens wanting to talk to their parents about finance, only 36% of adults actually feel qualified to discuss it."*

5 people determine your financial future

Robert Kiyosaki points out in support of this that the 5 people we spend most time with will give a good indication of where our money set-point is. Generally these 5 people determine your financial future in that you will not do things that will require you to depart from the rules (stated or not) of that group.

How does this happen in the brain? Can we override it? How?

Consider the following thoughts from T. Harv Eker (author of 'Secrets of The Millionaire Mind'):

"Each of us has an inner money 'thermostat' already engrained in our unconscious mind. It is the setting of this financial thermostat, more than anything and everything else that will determine your financial life.

You can be the best business person, the best negotiator, the best marketer, the best salesperson, the best communicator, the best manager, the best at your job…

You can know every new technique and the most current strategies for real estate and stocks…

But if your inner money thermostat is not preset for a high level of success, you will never amass a large amount of money. And if by some stroke of luck or hard work you do, you'll somehow manage to lose it so your finances return to your internal set point.

Can I give you an example?

I'm sure you've heard of Donald Trump. Here's this multi-billionaire who loses everything and more. And yet two years later, he's got it all back again — and more!

Why? Because his money thermostat is set for high.

On the other side of the coin, we've all heard the stories of lottery winners. They win $5 million, $10 million, $50 million, even $100 million dollars. Yet five years later, virtually half of them are right back to where they started.

Why? Because their money thermostat is set for low.

If you want to make and keep wealth, you must adjust your money thermostat.

What Determines Your "Money Thermostat" Set Point?

Now you might be wondering how your money thermostat got set in the first place?

And the answer is… by the information or programming you received in the past. Especially programming you received when you were young and an open vessel to the messages given to you by parents, teachers, religious leaders, media, and culture.

Take culture. Isn't it true that certain cultures have a certain way of thinking and dealing with money, while other cultures have a completely different way?

Do children come out of the womb dealing with money in a certain way… or are they taught how to do it that way? The latter, of course. We were all taught how to "do" money - often by people who either didn't have a lot of it or had emotional issues, negative thinking or non-supportive habits around it.

Their ways of thinking and being were AUTOMATICALLY ingrained in us and became our natural way of thinking and being when it comes to money." (2)

Neuroscience is honing in on some of the mechanisms that allow our brain systems to manage us physically, emotionally and mentally. Most of our emotional responses, mental processes and physical responses happen automatically and are governed in a recognisable part of the brain often referred to as the 'reptilian brain', or the 'limbic system'. It is called the reptilian brain as it is the part of the brain that is common to humans and reptiles – i.e. it is the original brain that most animals share from evolution. Neuroscientists are calling it '*System 1*'.

This part of the brain is a wonder of efficiency and has the major function of protecting us from death. As such, it runs on 'autopilot' – a mode made up of processes that have been input and remembered at an unconscious level from pre-birth and continuing throughout our lifetimes.

When we refer to 'fight or flight' responses, we are referring to responses that spring from our limbic systems. In the days when humans were involved in a daily fight for resources and life with other animals, it was necessary for our brains to react quickly to threats – fight the sabre tooth tiger or run from it was a common dilemma. These days, we are less likely to encounter such threats, but still have the neat ability to perceive threats real or not, and to react without conscious thought. Very useful if a truck is bearing down on you as you cross the road, and perhaps not as useful, although still operational, if the threat is your boss seeking to motivate you to achieve more at work by setting up competition against your peers.

The point is that this system functions from what is known as implicit memory. Implicit memory has been formed from up to 10,000 hours of doing or practicing a certain pattern or behavior. Once practiced enough, the pattern becomes unconscious.

The parts of our brains used for rational thought and decision making are referred to by neuroscientists as '*System 2*'. Mainly located in the Pre Frontal Cortex, this system is used for 'slow thinking', and utilises a great deal of energy when in operation. Research suggests we are only able to use this part of our brain for around 2 hours per day, either in cumulative short bursts, or in larger blocks of time.

If we are able to use our 'slow thinking' logical, rational part of our brain for only 2 hours per day, what's happening the rest of the time? Enter

'*System 1*' – that's right, we are operating from 'autopilot', implicit, unconscious, quick thinking for most of our waking hours. Better hope what's in there is good information!

If your unconscious is not working towards getting you what you want, you can change it.

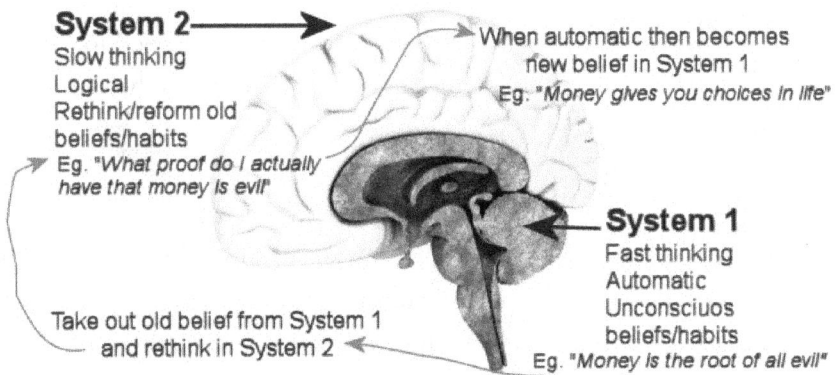

System 2⟶
Slow thinking
Logical
Rethink/reform old
beliefs/habits
Eg. *"What proof do I actually have that money is evil"*

When automatic then becomes new belief in System 1
Eg. *"Money gives you choices in life"*

System 1
Fast thinking
Automatic
Unconsciuos
beliefs/habits
Eg. *"Money is the root of all evil"*

Take out old belief from System 1 and rethink in System 2

Just like riding a bike – learning was initially difficult, but after much practice, there was not much need for conscious thought. Whilst learning, your brain was forging new pathways to enable you to remember how to ride. It was laying a path one way, then adding layers or changing it as you developed more finesse. This involved using all sections of the brain as rational thought to evaluate your progress. Finally, the pathway was so well laid and pruned of any unnecessary branches, that it became super efficient - implicit and unconscious.

To change a pattern that is so ingrained that you may not even know or remember where it came from can be hard, but not impossible. The first step is to recognise that what you are doing is not working the way you want it to.

This can be hard to acknowledge – we tend to tie up a lot of energy in hanging onto long held patterns of thought, emotion or behavior, and letting go can cause grief. Be prepared to grieve for the old pattern. The fact is, you are most likely giving up part of your innocence and childhood, as something like managing money wisely is more an adult concept, and it's hard to let go of our childlike fantasies.

After acknowledgement comes a willingness to forgive yourself for the time spent not getting what you want. After this you can calmly and without judgement examine what you've been doing vs alternatives that may serve you better.

When you find a better way, be willing to spend some time putting it into practice, until it is a new implicit memory. Remember it took up to 10,000 hours to get there, so your brain will need some time doing the new pattern consciously before the old pathways are over-ridden by the new. Some say you need at least 21 days to set up a new habit if practicing every day. If practicing once per week, you would need at least 21 weeks. Now, that's less than 10,000 hours, but if it's not totally new to you, you will already have some useful connections in your brain that just need strengthening and perhaps some new branches.

Getting back to how your 'money set point' is determined:

I don't believe it's useful for each of us to have a vague goal of having lots of money or being rich – this sets us up for disappointment and frustration – firstly if we don't manage to ever reach the goal, secondly if we do and don't feel the contentment and fulfilment that should come from the achievement. Our goals should be more about what makes us happy.

In an ideal world, we could all be happy and content if we each knew the unique gift we bring to the world and where able to freely contribute it, and have all of our needs met by the gifts given by each other. Of course this ideal world doesn't currently exist, so we use money instead as a unit of exchange and store of value to meet our needs. The system of money is not, however, perfect. Gross inequalities exist, partly because of circumstance, and partly because of the set point of our own internal 'money thermostats'.

How good is it then that we can each learn to re-set our internal 'money thermostats' to at least the amount of money that will fulfil all of our essential needs, and teach this to our children so that they start out life with a healthy set-point?

This is what this book is really all about. In it I explore what our essential needs are, how we can meet them, and most importantly, how we should learn from a young age to allocate money towards the fulfilment of each of them. Teaching our children to allocate in this way gets some useful autopilot, *System 1* patterns into their brain early and sets them up for a life of power, success and freedom with money.

Important Findings from Recent Studies of the Brain

Understanding the way our brains work, and how we learn, are crucial elements in teaching any topic. We are learning more and more everyday, and can apply our insights to improve our outcomes in life. Some findings from recent studies presented here, I believe, are key to success in teaching about money in our current day where the medium used to transact is mainly electronic, and the way we keep track of our money is also mainly online.

These studies are covered in Norman Doidge's bestselling book - '*The Brain That Changes Itself*'.

The first is a study by Marshall McLuhan who founded media studies in Canada in the 1950's and famously coined the phrase 'Global Village'. Another famous statement he made that is more relevant to our work here is *the medium is the message*. The argument is that each medium reorganizes our mind and brain in its own way. The consequences of these re-organisations are far more significant than the effects of the message.

Erica Michael and Marcel Just of Carnegie Melon University went on to prove via brain scan study that different brain areas are involved in hearing speech and reading it, and 'different comprehension centres' are activated in hearing words vs reading them.

Doidge argues that different circuits develop in the brain from different mediums.

McLuhan said that each medium leads to a change in the balance of our individual senses, and that imbalances occur. This does not prove that the increase in use of electronic mediums is harmful, however, there is evidence that harm comes from the effect on attention (more on this soon).

An experiment from a team at Hammersmith Hospital in London showed that *dopamine (a brain chemical that makes us feel good when rewarded. triggered in addiction) is released in the brain as children play typical computer games. Frequent dopamine hits allow us to maintain our focus and lose track of time and other resources (like rational thought and money) when playing our favourite computer game or slot machine.* (3)

These findings also don't prove that our increasing use of electronic media is harmful, until you make the link between the way our brains behave in light of these frequent dopamine hits and the way it behaves in addiction.

Other work which sheds light has been cited by Lieberman and Berkman in 2008. They were considering the distinctions between levels of mental abstraction, and how these activate in the brain (concrete representations tended to activate in the posterior regions and abstract in anterior regions).(4) An interesting observation was made by them in reference to the work of Wegner, Valacher and Dizadji in 1989, that *people who are alcoholics tend to represent drinking at more abstract levels than people who are not alcoholics, and this makes it very hard for them to break their drinking habit.*

Now stay with me here… Because what we can learn from these studies is extremely useful in determining how we should teach our children about money:

McLuhan stated '*the medium is the message*' i.e. how the message is conveyed affects how it is received. What medium do we use to learn about money today? Mainly electronic transactions and reports, and for children, what we tell them and what they observe us or other children saying and doing.

Michael and Just proved that different parts of the brain are activated when we hear words vs when we read words – i.e. different mediums activate different parts of the brain.

Doidge argued that different circuits in the brain develop in response to different mediums.

The team at Hammersmith Hospital showed that children engaged in computer games (i.e. delivering messages via an electronic medium), triggered the release of the same neurotransmitter that is released in addiction.

Lieberman and Berkman found that concrete representations (derived from actual sensory experience) activate a different part of the brain than where abstract representations activate.

Wegner, Valacher and Dizadji found that alcoholics represent drinking at more abstract levels than non-alcoholics – i.e. they don't experience their drinking as being real and having a detrimental affect on their health, so are able to continue drinking way past the point where non-alcoholics drink. Crucially, behavioral change is more difficult to affect if the memories of the experiences are represented at an abstract level.

Would you say that our concept of money these days is concrete or abstract?

What are possible consequences of experiencing money as an abstract concept?

What are the implications of this for our children and future generations?

If the medium used to convey a message is abstract rather than concrete, and you put this in the context of financial literacy, we may have a valid reason why our modern world population is not getting the lesson of money – the medium is more and more electronic and does not involve enough of the senses, and the medium presents money in an abstract form, making relevant courses of action (or goal pursuit) difficult to determine or achieve. Also, when dealing with an abstract concept that is difficult to understand, emotional responses such as confusion, frustration, fear and anger are easily attached to the subject of money.

My conclusion is that money is becoming more and more of an abstract concept in our world because we are no longer handling it physically. **We are no longer forging the concrete representations in our brains around money that we had when we did handle it physically.**

This argument forms the basis of my belief that we need to go back a few steps when teaching children about money. **We need to go back to using coins and notes with our children from an early age so that they have the experience of physically handling money.**

Three practical areas are covered in this book:

Number one: As human beings we have 6 main needs that, if satisfied in a healthy way, provide the basis of a great life. These needs play out every moment of every day in our thoughts, our feelings and our actions.

When we allocate money to the satisfaction of each of these needs and teach our children to do the same, we set ourselves and our children up for happy, fulfilling lives. The 6 needs are:

1. Being part of and contributing to a *community* that is cohesive, safe and fair.
2. Having the freedom to express our emotions spontaneously, live in the moment, and have *fun*.
3. Obtaining the status we seek in life and attaining the big things - pursuing our passions, buying *big toys*, achieving success in our endeavours.
4. Maintaining a true sense of connection with other *people* - understanding and feeling understood by our loved ones and greater humanity.
5. Being able to continue a love of *learning* throughout our lifetimes, to gain feedback on our progress in life, and having the information at hand to take the next step.
6. Having a *treasure* chest to fall back on so that our dreams are not thwarted, and we can move forward based on hope for the future.

Number two: Children should be introduced to handling actual cash from an early age so as to involve all of their senses, before progressing to learn how to handle money electronically in our increasingly cashless society. This is because involvement of the sense of touch makes money a concrete subject rather than an abstract concept. Research has shown that concrete learning follows and forms different pathways in our brains, and is crucial for children to learn practical tasks. By starting with cash, they have concrete representations of money to fall back on when they progress to using electronic methods of handling their money.

Number three: Children should be required to earn their allowance and can be involved in household chores from an early age. In the real world, until you have assets that can replace your earned income with investment income, you work for your money. The earlier children learn this, the more prepared they will be for life as adults.

"Academic qualifications are important and so is financial education. They're both important and schools are forgetting one of them."
Robert Kiyosaki

Part 2 - How Children Get Money
The Great Allowance Debate

I know there's a debate about allowances in the community – I've heard all sorts of theories and practices so I state my position here before we proceed.

Pay your children an allowance. It is essential that children are given cash to handle from an early age.

Ensure that your children are required to earn their allowance, not as a reward for good behavior, but so they can learn to become good money managers.

In our household, there are jobs that each of us is required to do to contribute to the well-being of the household that we don't pay an allowance for. These jobs tend to be taking responsibility for our own things, like packing our belongings away after use, keeping our rooms tidy, looking after our clothing and shoes etc. Jobs that are done for another member or all members of the household like cooking, washing up, cleaning communally used rooms, cleaning the car etc attract allowance. At the time of writing, our 7 year old earns her allowance by setting and clearing the table each night. She is also learning to stack and pack away the dishwashing, fold and put away towels, prepare vegetables for meals, clean out cupboards, put out rubbish, help clean the car, and other similar jobs to add to her allowance earning tasks.

How much allowance is also a hot topic at the kindy or school gate. Normal seems to range from $2 to $20 per week where I live, in Australia. My advice is to find out from parents of children of similar age to yours what the range is in your community, what is expected before payment, and then set the jobs you require done and the amount you will pay according to what you can afford. Don't be drawn into keeping up with the family next door who may pay more than you.

Older children can do more, so will earn more than your younger ones.

Always give out the allowance in various coins and/or notes so that your children handle it and allocate it physically.

A blast from the past

Remember when Dad and/or Mom brought home the pay packet in cash and kept a budget. You may not, but it was the way it was done as Industrialization took hold, and was still happening in some households right up until and into the 90's. For those of you old enough, you might remember seeing one of these …

Remember the weekly "paypacket" containing cash

Going back to the times when it was common for the family to have just one 'breadwinner' (usually Dad), they came home each week with a paypacket containing cash. The cash was then allocated – money for the housekeeping was usually given to Mom. Money for the bills was placed in marked envelopes and put aside until payment was due. Some of the cash was banked for savings and 'a rainy day'. Dad would put anything left over into his wallet to buy his daily newspaper or a bit of fun with his mates.

It was a simple system and as long as it was adhered to, it worked.

Teaching children to allocate their allowance can be just as simple.

How Do Children Currently Learn To Allocate Money?

If they learn at all, most put some in their piggy bank, and the rest in their purse, wallet or pocket. What happens if they run out of money in their purse or wallet – out comes the hammer and smash goes the piggy bank!

This is why piggy banks don't work!

Toolkit For Allowance Strategies

If you look online, there are some excellent systems on the market now to teach children to allocate money. Some include a money box with 4 compartments - Charity, Spending, Saving and Investing.

I believe we need to allocate to the 6 essential needs we all share, so have expanded the concept and created the Money Bags system. The Money Bags system is similar, but more comprehensive, and needn't involve a lot of expense to set up. You need 2 main tools:

1. Money 'Bags'

'Bags' can mean envelopes, snap lock plastic storage bags (zip bags), jars, plastic containers, even money boxes. Whatever suits you and whatever you have on hand. You can always change it later but the most important thing is to start. You will need 6 - one for each of the 6 essential needs.

Whatever 'bags' you choose, you'll want them to be tough enough to handle the cash (after all, you want the children to use them).

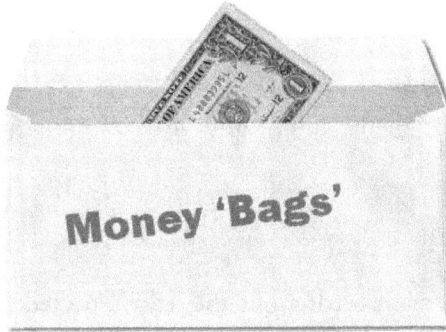

Label them as follows:

1. Community,

2. Fun,

3. Big Toys,

4. People,

5. Learning and

6. Treasure.

You also need a sturdy box to keep them in, like a shoe box, or plastic lunch box.

This is a great project for the children to get involved with, and as a bonus, we have made it even easier by preparing labels for your children to stick on each 'bag' - download from www.kidsmoneyrules.com when you join. Once the stickers are on, the children can decorate them however they like

- they might draw or stick on a picture for each one to remind them what the money is for. They can write or draw a picture of where the money from this envelope goes (e.g. in their wallet, to the bank, to their charity). And they can have fun decorating their 'money box' too.

On the following pages, I set out what each need ('Bag') is, ways to teach your children about them, and a guide to how much to allocate to each need.

2. The Help Chart

Next you'll need a chart setting out the help expected for an allowance to be earned, and how much is paid. You don't need to pay for each of these chores - decide which ones are expected as a member of the family, and which ones are extra and earn allowance money.

There are a number of ways to use the chart - you can make it a big chart and place it on a wall with markers nearby so that chores are marked off as they are done, or you could print it out on A4 as a list which is marked off by your child and presented to you each week at an appointed allowance time, or your children can make their own charts. We've presented an example chart for you to use on our website www.kidsmoneyrules.com.

You'll also find a great guide to the types of tasks that you can expect in each age group from popular parenting author Michael Grose by signing up for his newsletter, follow the link on our website www.kidsmoneyrules.com.

What If My Child Is NOT Motivated By Money?

Your child may not be all that interested in money. Especially if it means that they have to do chores to earn it. That's ok. It's like anything in life. A lack of attention to an important skill in life will show up somewhere sooner or later in life in the form of logical consequences:

- Failure to tidy up after oneself results in lost or damaged belongings
- Failure to follow rules at home and at school results in loss of freedom or privileges
- Failure to do chores results in no allowance

Your child may not be interested in money, but there will be something they are interested in that you can substitute until they are. It's what they want that money can buy them – toys, entertainment, brand name clothes, hobbies, treats etc.

Try substituting these as incentives to do their chores until they express interest in earning money and buying their own stuff instead.

Where Is Money Really Spent?

Now here's a concept (thanks to Robert Kiyosaki and Sharon Lechter) I'll refer to at times that is key to understanding and managing money. There are really only 3 places we spend money as adults:

- In the past
- In the present
- In the future

Money spent in the **past** is what we pay to our financiers – banks, credit providers, parents, even governments, for things we have enjoyed buying in the past. Not a good place to spend money unless it's to buy a home rather than rent it (rent being money spent in the present). Historically most homes have retained value over the long term, whilst most other things bought with credit have long lost all value by the time the loan is paid off.

Money spent in the **present** (or the now) is what we pay for our day to day living – food, water, power, fuel, entertainment, clothing etc. It includes money spent on credit but paid in full at the end of each month.

Money spent in the **future** is what we save and invest to spend on living in the future – either for large purchases, or to replace our income in retirement.

By allocating money to the 6 essential needs we all have, we are allocating money to the present and future, and learning how not to spend money on the past.

To sum up, here are some allowance tips:

- Allocate how much allowance you can afford to pay your children.
- Pay allowance consistently (pick a day and stick to it).
- Teach them what to do with their allowance (i.e. allocation to the 6 essential needs).
- Pay your children in mixed denominations of cash, notes and coins.

"If you only have a hammer, you tend to see every problem as a nail."
Abraham Maslow

Part 3 - The Six Essentials

Before we get into the how to information in this section, gather together your children in your mind's eye. Include your own inner child who may have missed some useful money lessons in the past. Give all of your children a big hug, and tell them you love them just for who they are. Tell them you love them so much and want them to have a fabulous life. Tell them you love them so much that you are willing to learn some new ways to manage money because you want them to have the best chance of success, freedom and power with money.

Now, let's get into the 6 essentials for allocation of money:

The 6 essentials for allocation of money are basic needs we all have. Much research across various areas of study in both Eastern and Western society has established these as the main 6. Brain research is now discovering the actual circuits, networks, and transmissions that support these needs in our human systems (brain, body, spirit).

"I'm a reflection of the community." Tupac Shakur

1. Community

What is this essential need?

Each of us has a primary need to belong to a community that sticks together, protects, and fairly enforces rules for the benefit of all. The way our communities function determines how our basic physiological needs are met. Only when this base is healthy can we go forward to fulfil the other needs we have in life in a healthy way.

All great communities are built on a foundation of 3 systems, or sets of rules – Our Legal system, Economic system, and Culture. Why not our families?

Think about how the rules of our society determine how our basic physiological and spiritual needs are met. We have family units to produce and nurture children, we have building codes to ensure that the roof over our head is structurally sound, we have food safety and handling regulations to ensure that the water and foods we eat are not poisonous, we have financial institutions to determine and manage the flow of money, we have religious and philosophical institutions to nurture our spirit.

Most of us become exhausted just thinking of all the institutions and regulations we live with, but why is it that we have these in the first place?

It's all about the need for us to feel we live in a society that is cohesive, fair and safe. In fact, if we don't feel this need is satisfied by our group of origin (i.e. the family, community, society we live in), we will actively seek a group we are comfortable with. Parents will move a child to a different school if the child is not feeling safe, teenagers and young adults will join gangs if they feel the rules of their family don't suit them, people move locations in search of a community they are happy to be a part of.

Each group in society will have rules (implicit or explicitly stated) for how to belong in that group – consider your family, workplace, church, school, hobby group etc. What are some of the rules of your group? And what happens when the rules are broken? Punishment can be swift and painful – temporary or more permanent removal from the group. Members are often gouged out and made to feel that they don't belong.

If you've ever been the last one picked in the playground or in school sports for a team, you'll know what social pain feels like.

INTERESTING BRAIN STUDY

Naomi Eisenberger, Matthew Lieberman and their colleagues, Neuroscientists at University of California Los Angeles, in the 'Cyberball Studies' (5), show that in the brain, social pain (i.e. that caused by perceived exclusion from a group) shows up in some of the same regions as physical pain. This pain can be alleviated by the same pain killing drugs that are used to alleviate physical pain!

We naturally seek to maximize pleasure and avoid pain, and avoiding social pain is the motive of an infant just separated from its mother by the birthing process. Those cries soon settle when baby is re-united with Mom.

Brain research is refuting Maslow's well known Hierarchy of Needs, and placing 'Belonging' firmly at the base of the pyramid, ahead of Biological and Physiological needs.

The reason we seek to fulfil this need first is that it ensures our survival from the moment we are conceived. We come into the world totally dependent on someone else (our primary caregiver, most often our mother). Our primary caregiver is dependent on those around her or him to keep them safe and healthy whilst they care for the new child. The rules of belonging are encrypted into our being well before we even have words to describe them.

Studies that prove this concept are compelling:

Anthony De Casper and Melanie Spence concluded after their 1986 controlled study of new borns (6), that we are predisposed to recognize our mother's voice because we are able to hear it in-utero in the 3rd trimester of pregnancy. Newborns who had been exposed to their mother's voice in-utero with a regular reading of a specific passage of prose, were shown to prefer their mother's reading of the passage soon after birth over a random female voice. Newborns who had not been exposed to the regular reading in-utero showed no specific preference.

In addition, the long running and ongoing Bucharest Early Intervention Project which involves children abandoned at or around the time of birth and placed in one of 6 institutions for young children in Bucharest, Romania in the late nineties, has changed the approach taken in the developed world to institutionalizing orphans.

'Under Ceausescu, child abandonment became a national disaster, as families could not afford to keep their children, and were encouraged to turn more than 100,000 of them over to the state.

Children raised in institutions are at dramatically increased risk for a variety of social and behavioral abnormalities, including:

- Disturbances and delays in social/emotional development
- Aggressive behavior problems
- Inattention/hyperactivity
- Syndrome that mimics autism*
- Developmental problems believed to result from deprivation inherent in institutional care

    *…which disappears once a child is adopted.' (7)

The study proves that deprivation of normal family structure in infancy and early childhood causes serious developmental issues for children. The children who were taken out of institutional care and placed in high quality foster care prior to age 2 were able to significantly overcome these issues. The study concluded that the earlier the child is placed with a caring family, the better.

Why Is This Relevant To Teaching Children About Money?

Within our communities, we each have certain roles to play. These we learn from a very early age, and the roles we adopt give each of us our sense of who we are in the group, and how we contribute to the overall well-being of the community.

Firstly, what is your role as a parent – are you raising a child who will be forever dependent on you and society, or an adult who learns to be responsible for them self and is able to contribute to the well-being of the community as a whole?

Of course, when our children are infants, they need lots of attention so that they feel safe. As they develop and begin to explore their world, they need rules and boundaries to keep them feeling safe. As they develop into adolescence and adulthood, the boundaries are loosened off and/or changed to reflect the new areas of life they are exploring, and they become more and more bound by the community's rules. Family rules, attitudes, values and behavior will remain with them until they are able to mindfully examine them as adults if they so choose.

The point is, our children pick up on our money attitudes, values and practices whether we explicitly teach them or not.

The way we relate to and manage money is an important section of the roles we adopt, and the rules or code of conduct within each of our families.

We may not think about it often, but each of us has taken on money lessons we learned from our parents, peers and society. Some of us have taken the time to examine these roles and rules and decide which of them are useful to us, and which can be replaced by roles and rules that suit us better. If you haven't done this yet, it's never too late to change them with some conscious effort.

Here's a quick and easy test to give you instant insight into your current beliefs about money:

What's your first reaction when you come across someone who obviously has a lot of money? (*Write it down.*)

The reactions can range from '*good on them*', to '*they must have done something dodgy*', to '*I deserve more than them*' to '*what can I learn from them?'* etc. What was your reaction? Do you think it is healthy? Could it be replaced by something more useful to you and your family?

Secondly, we each have a vested interest in ensuring that we have a healthy community that gives each member of it a fair chance to succeed.

INTERESTING BRAIN STUDY

Golnaz Tabibnia and Matthew Lieberman conducted a review (8) of recent brain based studies related to fairness and cooperation in 2007. They found that our brain system recognises fair or cooperative behavior in a different region to unfair and uncooperative behavior. Fair behavior is rewarded by positive feelings stemming from dopamine release in the ventral striatum (associated with positive reinforcement), and unfair behavior is discouraged by feelings of disgust stemming from the ventral insular.

In our society, financial success is not possible for some people due to circumstances beyond their control, and this not always fair. Our tax systems may provide funding to partially support us when we are unable to do so ourselves, but we also have various institutions set up to help those of us in serious difficulty. You can influence and enhance the health of your community by committing some of your money to these institutions. These can include charities, political parties, religious institutions, educational facilities etc. It is important that we support these institutions for the good of the community as a whole. Your cooperation and effort to redress unfairness is a physiological need rewarded in your brain.

10% of the sales proceeds of this book are dedicated to charities in my local community, national community and international community for projects that aid individuals to financial success in those communities. I've set this up for the good of these institutions, but also to satisfy my need to be part of a healthy community and undo some of the unfairness that exists in our world.

Some of us are so generous that we would give the shirt off our back to someone in need of it. On the surface, this is commendable, but not if we then become needy ourselves. If you find it hard to say no to someone in need, and regularly find yourself giving more than you intended, or can afford, here are some tips to set up your giving as an automatic system:

- Decide how much of your income you will give – 10% is a common amount
- Research and select 2 or 3 causes that resonate with who you are or that you feel passionately about
- Divide your chosen amount amongst them (i.e. if you chose to give away 10% of your income to 3 charities, give 3.33% to each, not 10% to each)
- Set up a regular way to pay your donations – most causes are able to accept direct credits these days, so you could set up a direct debit from your transaction account

A big advantage of this method is that once you have your system set up, it is easier to say no to the various other requests you receive for assistance from other causes that are not as dear to your heart. You can with good conscience reply to the next request "I'd love to help, but our giving program has already been decided."

Now, another way to view community is as a launching pad where you feel safe enough to go forward and find fulfilment for your other needs. A healthy launch pad will have just enough rules to give a sense of safety without feeling overly controlled or that there is no solid base to start from.

As a parent, you know that your children need boundaries, but they don't respond well to being controlled to within an inch of their lives. A good set of family rules is key to setting up your children to be great members of their community.

Some of the rules in your home will apply to the way the family conducts itself generally, as well as in the context of money. A key concept that applies generally and specifically when it comes to money is being trustworthy. A rule such as:

"My word is my bond" is a great starting place. For younger children, learning this rule starts with rules forbidding lying and cheating. Often young children view money as a shiny play object and don't get that it has value as currency for the family to be able to have what it wants and needs. Making this clear from an early age will set your children up for an honest relationship with money throughout their lifetimes.

For young children this starts with learning to put things away after using them, taking care not to break things, cleaning up, taking care with the belongings of others and returning them after use or play.

Children like to play with money. Playing games with real money is great, as long as children know where the money comes from (i.e. who owns it), and that the money is to be returned there afterwards unless it is given as a gift (i.e. it changes ownership). Handling an allowance is a great way for children to play with notes and coins.

The key learning point here is that we value and look after our money so that we are able to have all of the things we need in our lives without having to rely on others to provide for us.

A more specific money rule is:
"Money is not easy come easy go - it is earned from effort of some kind"

Occasionally we receive money because of circumstances beyond our control such as gifts, good luck, social security or the death of a loved one.

For most of us, the money we have is gained through personal exertion. It may be easier for some to make money than others, and some may enjoy their exertion more than others, but the principle holds true whether you enjoy the process or not. (Finding ways to enjoy your work is a subject for another book).

Teaching children this rule starts with having an allowance system in your home that rewards effort on assigned tasks with money.

As children get older, they can find ways to supplement their allowance through enterprises of their own, and part time jobs.

Here's a great rule that is a wealth creator from the get go:
"Pay yourself first"
It means that from every dollar you earn, from day 1, you put the money you need for yourself in future aside as savings for fulfilment of your goals. Some goes into a savings account for a buffer and shorter term goals, and some goes towards investments for the day when you can choose to work or not. Open 2 savings accounts each for your children - 1 for short term savings, and 1 for money that will be invested.

And of course, there is the Golden Rule of Money:
"Spend no more than you earn"
When you spend more than you earn, you are in debt.

Spending more than we earn reached epidemic proportions in western world households in the lead up to the Global Financial Crisis. As home prices rose above their real value, and homeowners felt secure in their jobs, banks offered credit in the form of home equity loans, credit card limit increases, and easy to get personal loans. Consumers used this easy money to buy anything and everything they wanted, often without sufficient thought given to how they would pay the money back, or how much debt they were really in.

Banks offered loans to people who, in normal economic conditions, would never qualify for credit, and they spent up big too.

In the Global Financial Crisis, households where brought to account (many losing their homes), corporations that where overextended went broke taking investors down with them, and our governments were forced to spend more than they were earning in order to bail out the banks that lent the money.

A simple rule, 'spend no more than you earn', if it was followed by each household, corporation and government could have prevented the GFC!

What do you think of the example rules I've presented here? What are your family's rules about money? How do they compare to your community's rules about money? Do you feel safe being part of the family that follows these rules? If not, what new rules would you like to have in your family?

What role do you play in managing your family's money? If you have a partner, do you and your partner share this role, or is it left up to one of you? Are you the spender? The saver? The teacher? I address managing money in the family in a later chapter.

Teaching Community to Children

1. **First, set a good example.** Examine your own story around money and change what is no longer useful to you. This is top priority, as your children learn by copying you.

For some of you, this will be easy – simply recognizing what's not working for you will be all that's needed to spur you on to find a better set of rules and processes. For others, this will be more difficult, especially if you have a lot of emotional energy tied up in the way you do things now. It's possible that you won't even know how this 'angst' has come to be part of you (remember that many of our implicit memories are formed before we develop language and rational thought). Thankfully, there are many resources available to you, both paid and free of charge, which can help you unlock and get past the unconscious barriers to your financial learning and progress. These include training courses, coaching, counseling, meditation, hypno-therapy, and psychology.

You may be thinking I'm not into that 'airy-fairy psycho-babble' stuff, and this is a valid reaction. But I ask you – how well is your current unconscious way of handling money serving you? Surely, finding a better, less stressful way to manage yourself around money will be a great boost in your life and worth a small investment of time, effort and even some money.

One of the easiest methods I've found to unlock and move past unconscious patterns is called Emotional Freedom Technique or EFT (also known as Tapping). You can access this method via professionals in your area, via self-help books, and on the web. www.tappingsolution.com is a great place to start if you want to explore how this method can help you.

Also, by reading this book, you are developing new techniques to be more financially mindful and make better financial decisions.

2. **It is important for you to have regular healthy discussions about money with your children** - how you earn your money (if you can, take them to work with you from time to time), your role in handling the family's finances, how money is used to enable the family to meet its needs and the needs of the community, what you have learned from your own family that is useful, as well as mistakes you may have made in the past.

Here's a Family Meeting agenda re money rules that you might like to use:

Existing rules	Keep, Replace, or Remove	Replacement Rule	Review by *(date)*
General rules that also apply to money *E.g. My word is my bond*			
Specific money rules *E.g. Spend less than you earn*			

3. **Set up and implement an allowance system.** Be consistent with following your system.

4. **Regularly discuss with your children the charities you support and why.** You can also add in the concept of the role of government and taxation. Some families take tax from allowances and use it for a common family or community goal.

Encourage them to find a cause that they are happy to support themselves. Make it a fun research project and use their school, media and the internet for ideas.

5. **Decide an amount they can allocate out of their allowance to their Community money bag.** As a guide, many families allocate 10%.

6. **Encourage them to decorate their Community 'Money Bag'** with a picture representing the cause they have chosen.

Help them to regularly donate this money to their chosen cause.

7. **Encourage them to draw a diagram for or write on their Community 'Money Bag' how the money they place in this bag gets to their chosen cause** (e.g. taken each month and deposited in the Charity Box at the supermarket, given to Mom each month to send off to the charity, deposited to a bank account for electronic transfer to the cause).

Action Plan:

Write down the tips from this section you plan to implement with your own family. Add any additional ideas that come to mind. Make a note of who is responsible for each item, and when it will be actioned.

"Poetry is when an emotion has found its thought and the thought has found words." Robert Frost

2. Fun

What is this essential need?

We each have a need to express our emotions (whether we acknowledge this or not).

I've labeled this need fun, but of course, there are a huge range of emotions we express throughout our day. When we express emotion, we are signaling to ourselves or others that we have needs that we want met – fear, hurt, hunger, lust, frustration, anticipation, love, appreciation, happiness, joy are just some of the range of emotions we are capable of expressing.

When we are able to freely express our emotions we become child-like and vulnerable. It is important for us to feel we are in a safe environment before we express freely. The health of our community plays a huge part in how we express emotion. The rules (both explicit and implicit) make it very clear if it is ok or not to express ourselves, how we should express ourselves, which emotions are ok to express or not and even when it is ok to be emotional.

INTERESTING BRAIN STUDY

For over one hundred years, talk therapies have been practiced as a way to clear negative emotions. The assumption is that by labeling the emotion, and talking about our feelings, the impact of the emotion will be diminished in current experience. Commonly referred to as affect labeling, the practice of labeling one's emotions by talking about them or writing them down has been shown by observation to be effective, but the actual brain mechanisms that were at work where not available to see until recently.

Using FMRI, the team at UCLA have shown that labeling our emotions works to settle down our limbic system and clear the pathway for us to engage our Pre Fontal Cortex to apply reasoning to a situation rather than rely on our habitual response. (9)

The presence of emotion allows our system to access behavioral memory which resides in our brains in the limbic system (*System 1*). If we are able to express our emotions in a healthy way, impulses in our pleasure and pain centres (mainly our limbic system) inform the mid brain which instructs the body including priming or relaxing muscles according to previous experience of the emotion, releasing appropriate hormones and neurotransmitters; and interacting with the pre-frontal cortex to formulate new plans and actions if the current set don't achieve the desired outcome (i.e. reasoning or *System 2*). Here's that diagram of the brain again.

System 2
Slow thinking
Logical
Rethink/reform old
beliefs/habits
Eg. "What proof do I actually
have that money is evil"

When automatic then becomes
new belief in System 1
Eg. "Money gives you choices in life"

System 1
Fast thinking
Automatic
Unconsciuos
beliefs/habits
Eg. "Money is the root of all evil"

Take out old belief from System 1
and rethink in System 2

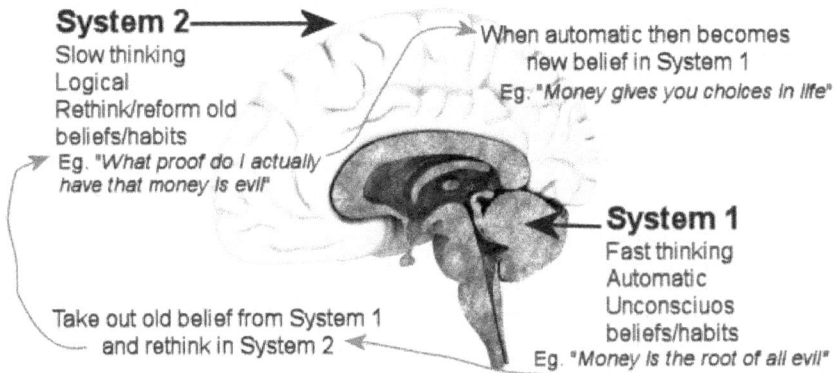

If we are not able to express in a healthy way, the emotion is not cleared from our limbic system. (System 1)

The effect on our brain when emotion is not cleared from the pleasure and pain centres is to decrease cognitive ability (i.e. our ability to reason). If not cleared, our experience of life may be impaired in some way as our automatic responses don't solve our problems.

We often use money to help us clear emotions in the form of retail therapy, and this is fun sometimes, but not if it is out of control and racking up huge credit card bills.

The key to good money management here is in determining ahead of time what is spent on needs vs wants. Determining what a need is and what is a want can be tricky. What is necessary expenditure and what is not? Satisfying hunger by buying and preparing nutritious food is necessary expenditure, but what about that sugary snack – is that used to satisfy hunger (in which case it's a need), or some other emotion (in which case you could argue that the food is a want used to satisfy a different type of need)? How else could that need be satisfied?

We face such decisions every day and sorting out needs from wants for ourselves is hard enough without helping our children with similar dilemmas.

The key is to simply put a name to the emotion we are feeling when we feel the urge to shop. It's not something we are used to doing. In fact, we don't tend to have a lot of labels for the vast array of emotions we feel. Consider the range that could be included under the umbrella of 'anger' – rage, annoyance, frustration are some within the range, but we just call it anger. The closer we can get to the actual emotion we are feeling, the more affect we can have on diminishing its hold on us.

Learning to delay gratification is a key learning for success in life (including financial success).

A famous study that began in the 1960's proves that those of us who have learned to delay gratification will be more successful than those of us who have not (and this includes success with managing money).

The 'Marshmallow Experiment' has been widely cited in relation to personality and psychology. Jonah Lehrer brought information up to date on this ongoing research in The New Yorker, in May 2009 in his article 'Don't! The Secret of Self Control'.

The initial study was conducted in the 60's and 70's at the Bing Nursery School, on the campus of Stanford University with a group of children around age 4. The experiment was designed and presided over by Professor of Psychology, Walter Mischel. Initially, Mischel set out to identify the mental processes that allowed some people to delay gratification while others gave in.

Children were asked to enter a games room containing nothing much more than a desk and chair. On the desk was a treat the child had selected (most children chose a marshmallow) and a bell. A researcher made each child an offer – they could eat the marshmallow straight away, or if they were willing to wait a few minutes whilst the researcher stepped out of the room, they could have 2 marshmallows on his return. If the child chose to eat the marshmallow, they were to ring a bell and the researcher would come back straight away so the child could eat the marshmallow, but they would forfeit the second one.

Most of the children struggled with their emotions and gave in within 30 seconds. But 30% were able to hold out for 15 minutes and wait for the greater reward. They had found ways to distract themselves from the immediate treat in return for more, such as singing to themselves, looking away from the treat, playing under the desk etc.

Mischel's own children attended the Bing Centre, so he was able to check in on how the children in the experiment were faring as they grew older by asking after certain of them that remained friends with his own children during school. He started to notice some patterns in their relative success at school that prompted him to check further.

In the early 80's Mischel conducted further research with the parents, educators and advisors of the children involved in the earlier study.

The results were surprising and extended across a range of indicators including academic success as well as behavior. The low-delayers (those children who were not able to hold out for greater reward) seemed to be having more problems with achieving success at school and at home than the high-delayers.

Mischel and his colleagues continued to track the participants into their 30's, and Mischel recently initiated further studies using fMRI scanning. He argues that intelligence is largely at the mercy of self control - "What we're really measuring with the marshmallows isn't will power or self-control," Mischel says. "It's much more important than that. This task forces children to find a way to make the situation work for them. They want the second marshmallow, but how can they get it? We can't control the world, but we can control how we think about it." Read more at www.newyorker.com.

INTERESTING BRAIN STUDY

Wikipedia reports the results of the fMRI scan study as follows: "A 2011 study of the same participants indicates that the characteristic remains with the person for life. Additionally, brain imaging showed key differences between the two groups in two areas: the prefrontal cortex (more active in high delayers) and the ventral striatum (an area linked to addictions)."

Why Is This Relevant To Teaching Children About Money?

Expressing emotion is the area where we spend most of our money. It is where we satisfy what we want or need in the here and now – for example:

- Safety – a roof over our heads
- Hunger – food on our tables
- Fun – entertainment, toys, excursions, 'retail therapy', hobbies
- Comfort – clothing, heating, cooling
- Loneliness – entertaining others, sharing experiences, pets

It is easy to get carried away with expenditure in this area. A lot of our problems with debt arise because of emotional spending (too much money spent in the now becomes money spent in the past). Overspending here can be one of the learned behaviors that are an automatic reaction to certain emotional states, which is stored in the limbic system. If the triggering emotions are not cleared, access to reasoning is limited. One way of clearing the emotions that trigger over-spending is to notice the emotion, label it, and delay action – learning to distract yourself is a major key to success.

There can also be a lot of judgment – both self judgment and judgment by others brought to bear about emotional expenditure, derived from the rules of your family of origin and your community. It can be ok to express some emotions and not others. Spending on satisfying our daily needs for nourishing food, clean water, shelter, and basic clothing is seen as essential expenditure, whereas spending on having fun can be seen as frivolous.

In the broader context, unnecessary emotional expenditure produces waste, and waste has become a huge problem on our planet.

Again, exploring what your own rules are about expression of emotion and how this translates into expenditure is a very useful thing to do. Set up a 'safe zone' in your home for expression of emotion, and recognize that we spend money on satisfaction of emotional needs. When you delay action, you can make decisions about your expenditure here that serve you rather than enslave you.

Spending money on 'fun' can and should be fun. And it is with appropriate rules and limits in place. Make sure you have a budget that realistically covers your emotionally based living expenses. The majority of most household income is spent here – a healthy percentage to aim for is 50%. Have fun spending within your budget without guilt or regret.

Teaching "Fun" to Children

Did I really say 'teaching fun to children'?

OK - what I mean is teaching children how to express their emotions in ways that serve them rather than hinder their success in life. And that extends to learning to become aware of emotional expenditure.

1. **Children need to learn that living in the now costs money** - eating, running a car, heating/cooling, hot water, light, cleaning, TV, entertainment, clothing. Some of this expenditure is necessary, and some is for wants. Delaying gratification allows for more of what we want in future because we can save money for later. Often we rouse on our children for waste, for constant demands, for breaking house rules such as snacking before dinner, but how often do we sit down and discuss with them why we are upset with them?

We want our children's brains to develop the links associated with reasoning and delayed gratification when it comes to money, rather than unhelpful addictive links associated with impulsive behavior.

Help children to do this by:
- Teaching them to label their emotions, so they learn to calm their emotional systems and use their rational brains.
- Sharing with them how much money could be saved if they reduce waste, wait for what they want, and follow house rules designed for greater reward (e.g. a nutritious dinner rather than a sugary snack).
- Involving them when you are paying bills - explain what the bill is for, how you are paying for it (e.g. by check, at the counter, online) from your own money.

2. **Ask them how the household could save money on its regular bills.** Explain that you aim to keep your day-to-day living expenses to 50% of your income. Ask them for their ideas on how the family can save money so that you can achieve this and have money for other important needs.

Make it real by tracking some of the savings and putting it as cash into a jar. This needn't be complicated - just choose 3 things to track and put a price on them e.g.

- Turning off a light when not in use saves (say) a dime
- Choosing not to eat a snack before dinner saves (say) $1
- A shopping expedition with no demands for anything that's not on the list earns (say) $2

A simple tally sheet can be set up to track the savings each day, and then the money added to the jar each week. Choose as a reward a fun outing for all the family to enjoy, or a special treat like a family block of chocolate to share, then when there's enough in the jar, go get the reward.

3. **When out for a meal, offer the children that if they choose to drink water rather than a costly soda or juice, you will pay them the amount saved in cash.**

4. **When the children are shopping with their own money challenge them to find ways to make their money go further:**

How many pieces of candy can they get with one coin? Where are 3 places they could go to buy the same or a similar item and where will they pay the least? How many different ways can they find to buy the same or a similar item (e.g. shops, direct mail, online)?

5. **To help children understand how "fun" needn't cost a lot** and also let them see how some fun translates into money, here's an activity to try.

FUN FLOWER EXERCISE: Ask the children to draw a flower with 6 petals. On each petal, they can write in or draw a picture to represent things they love to do. Now ask them which ones cost money? Help them to determine if each one costs a small amount or a large amount and draw big or little money signs next to them. In most cases you will find that the things children love to do don't cost a lot of money, and that they have plenty of choice when it comes to inexpensive fun things to do.

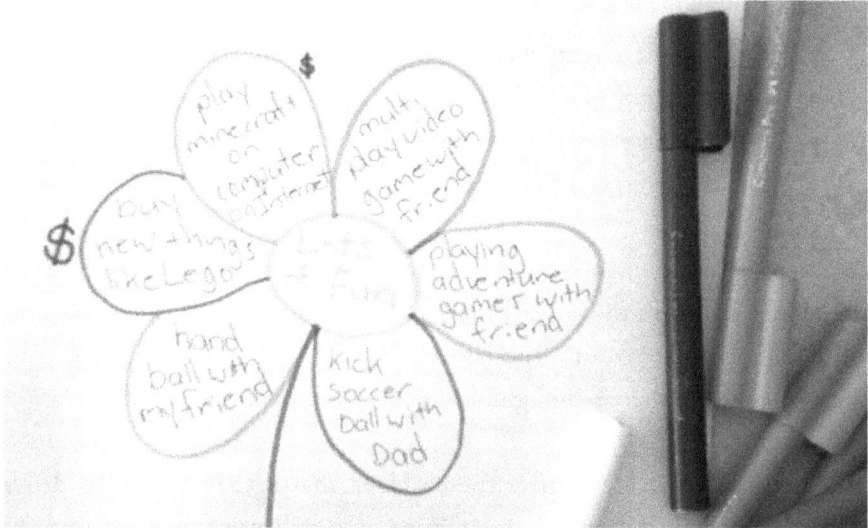

6. **Make sure they decorate their Fun bag with pictures of things that represent fun to them**, and a diagram to show where this money goes (i.e. into their purse or wallet for spending).

Action Plan:
Write down the tips from this section you plan to implement with your own family. Add any additional ideas that come to mind. Make a note of who is responsible for each item, and when it will be actioned.

"What you get by achieving your goals is not as important as what you become by achieving your goals." Henry David Thoreau

3. Big Toys

This is about our need for status. What's status? Other words that substitute for status are rank, eminence, prestige, standing and category. Generally status comes down to how you view yourself and how others view you in society – are you one of those seen to have power or not? Are you seen as a leader or not?

The word power, when applied to humans, carries connotations – when used to power over others, it is bullying.

Learning to have power within and power with is the key, and those who master this gain greater and more lasting status in our society. They are the leaders we look up to.

All of us are leaders in our own way – we are masters of our own destinies.

With a healthy sense of community in place, and a healthy expression of emotion in place, you have the basis from which to set out on your own to achieve what you want to achieve in life. Who are you as a leader in your family, community, society? What kind of leader do you want to be?

As you lead yourself on your own life's journey, there will be trophies to collect along the way. These are anything that displays your idea of status in the world - it may be your home, your car, your pursuit of a costly hobby, wearing expensive clothing, travelling first class, the corner office, the big pay cheque, collections – I call these your 'big toys'.

Being the leader of yourself requires setting up internal boundaries of what is ok and what is not ok for you to do, be, have – i.e. your values.

When it comes to spending money here, the purchases are those that you have gone without in the past so that you can have them now – in other words you have put in the hard yards and saved for them in some way. They are the expensive things you buy or attain because you value them for the pleasure you gain from them and can pat yourself on the back on the achievement. You are happy to share that pleasure with others or just with yourself.

Often the sharing of your pleasure in your achievements and your big toys inspires others to improve the way they lead their lives – what better outcome than to share the power you have within yourself with others.

I was listening to ABC Australia radio in the car recently and heard a great quote – I don't recall who was speaking or who they were quoting but it was along the lines – '*What do you do when you have reached your Mt Everest? You lean down and extend your hand to help others to achieve theirs.*' I think that truly encapsulates what it is to have power within and with others, and to be a leader with status in our society.

I love this excerpt from Sarah Ban Breathnach's book '*Simple Abundance Daily Comfort Book*':

Authentic Success

Authentic success is different for each of us. No single definition fits all because we come in all sizes. One autumn afternoon years ago, while wandering through an abandoned cemetery, I discovered a wonderful definition of authentic success inscribed on the headstone of a woman who died in 1820: "The only pain she ever caused was when she left us."

"Authentic success is having time enough to pursue personal pursuits that bring you pleasure, time enough to make the loving gestures for your family you long to do, time enough to care for your home, tend your garden, nurture your soul. Authentic success is never having to tell yourself or those you love, "maybe next year." Authentic success is knowing that if today were your last day on earth, you could leave without regret. Authentic success is feeling focused and serene when you work, not fragmented. It's knowing that you've done the best that you possibly can, no matter what circumstances you faced; it's knowing in your soul that the best you can do is all you can do, and that the best you can do is always enough.

Authentic success is accepting your limitations, making peace with your past, and revelling in your passions so that your future may unfold according to a Divine Plan. It's discovering and calling forth your gifts and offering them to the world to help heal its ravaged heart. It's making a difference in other lives and believing that if you can do that for just one person each day, through a smile, a shared laugh, a caress, a kind word, or a helping hand, blessed are you among women.

Authentic success is not just money in the bank but a contented heart and peace of mind. It's earning what you feel you deserve for the work you do and knowing that you're worth it. Authentic success is paying your bills with ease, taking care of all your needs and the needs of those you love, indulging some wants, and having enough left over to save and share. Authentic success is not about need. Authentic success is feeling good about who you are, appreciating where you've been, celebrating your achievements, and honoring the distance you've already come. Authentic success is reaching the point where being is as important as doing. It's the steady pursuit of a dream. It's realizing that no matter how much time it takes for a dream to come true in the physical world, no day is ever wasted. It's valuing inner, as well as outer, labor - both your own and others'. It's elevating labor to a craft and craft to an art by bestowing Love on every task you undertake.

Authentic success is knowing how simply abundant your life is exactly as it is today. Authentic success is being so grateful for the many blessings bestowed on you and yours that you can share your portion with others.

Authentic success is living each day with a heart overflowing."

Why Is This Relevant To Teaching Children About Money?

Sooner or later, children become conscious of status. Often it is as a result of peer pressure in the school yard, but it will be evident in the family too.

In a money sense, this is a lot about delayed gratification (remember the marshmallow test from last chapter). It's about having a personal goal and setting out to achieve it. For children, it's about being able to have the 'big toys' due to their own self-leadership efforts.

Status is earned, not bought.

Teaching Children About Status

1. Discuss with your children **how you came to obtain the big toys** you have in your life.

2. Teach children to **set smart goals:**

- **S**pecific - the goal needs to be described as if it were here right now. What is it? What does it look like? If I was from Mars, how would you explain what it is to me?
- **M**easurable - how will you know that you've achieved the goal? Can you measure steps along the way?
- First step **A**chievable - can you think of the first thing you need to do to make progress towards your goal? Can you do this step?
- **R**ealistic - is this something that you can actually get? Are you allowed to have it?
- **T**imebound - set a date that you expect you will reach your goal by.

3. Teach children to **develop their own sense of money power within by setting savings goals** for the big items they want. Reward them for finding additional ways to make the money they need (within the rules and with a strong value set) e.g. taking on more at home, seeking odd jobs to do in the neighbourhood, getting a part time job after school.

4. Set up a **savings chart for younger children**, or perhaps a spreadsheet for older children. Encourage them to place a picture of their goal on the chart, and to regularly fill in how they are progressing. When you subscribe at our website www.kidsmoneyrules.com you will receive some great savings chart tools.

5. Consider encouraging them in their efforts by **matching their savings**, or offering to contribute to their savings *rather than* purchasing something else they want that you were willing to buy.

6. When they have reached their goal, **celebrate - help them to actually purchase the object of their savings effort** as soon as possible. Encourage them to share the big toy and especially the story of how they got it and how that made them feel with their friends.

WARNING: It is easy for the goal to take over and for all their money to go towards it, so remind them to continue allocating for the other important needs whilst saving. I recommend 10-20% be allocated to 'Big Toys'.

7. Encourage them to decorate their Big Toys bag with pictures of the big toys or achievements they are aiming for. Have them draw a diagram of where this money goes (e.g. into a savings account).

Action Plan:
Write down the tips from this section you plan to implement with your own family. Add any additional ideas that come to mind. Make a note of who is responsible for each item, and when it will be actioned.

"Empathy is born out of the old biblical injunction 'Love thy neighbor as thyself.'" George McGovern

4. People

We each need to *connect* with other people and feel genuinely understood.

Neuroscientists have studied the way we connect with each other from 2 main viewpoints - some have discovered and researched what are known as 'mirror neurons' in the brain (and throughout our bodies). The mirror neuron system helps us to understand other people by feeling what they feel. Others have come at it from a field known as 'Theory of Mind', where a best guess is made of what another person is thinking, and this is tested against reality. If it matches, the other person may feel understood. More recently, studies have linked the 2 in an effort to better understand the brain's mechanisms for understanding the thoughts and feeling of others, and feeling understood and supported by others. When this need is met, our system is flooded with feel good hormones - oxytocin and vasopressin, we suspend judgment of others, and increase our willingness to give of ourselves.

Another name for genuine connection is empathy. Many of us sense that the world's way of distributing resources and delivering products and services for consumption in recent history has lacked empathy, and that humanity is now calling out for a more empathic way of meeting the needs of all human beings whilst also managing our footprint on the Earth. Our children will be heavily involved in finding new ways to distribute the planets' resources with empathy.

Meeting this need in a healthy way is crucial to the forming of healthy relationships with other people – friendships, partnerships, marriages, children. It is also why we are able to work with others in effective teams – by understanding each other's strengths and weaknesses, we can each work from our own unique talent bases to produce a much better result than if working alone.

We are naturally drawn to spending money on those we love or are closely connected to - money spent to have quality time with them, thoughtful gifts, ceremonies and celebrations of relationships (e.g. dates, engagements, weddings, honeymoons, family holidays, christenings, birthday parties, catching up with friends, workplace social club occasions etc).

The Beatles sang "Money can't buy me love", but I would argue that there are some things we like to buy to promote or signify our love – gifts, engagement and wedding rings ("Diamonds are a girl's best friend"…), ceremonies and celebrations to name a few.

Parents often save for their children's weddings, and children often contribute too. The cost of dating and gifts is usually born by the couple themselves.

An interesting trend has emerged in recent years that puts weddings in the realm of status rather than connecting with people – it seems the more you spend on your children's weddings, the more status you enjoy. When people are genuinely connected, there's no need to overspend on the public demonstration of that connection.

And here's another trend – long distance relationships. We are so easily able to connect with people from all over the planet now, and to fall in love with someone who lives on the other side of the world. Sooner or later connecting over the internet doesn't cut it and travel becomes a necessary cost of maintaining the relationship.

The most important consideration here is that genuine connection with others starts with love of oneself – the more we love and appreciate ourselves, the better we are able to connect with others and contribute our unique talents to the world.

Speaking of connection - are you and your partner really connecting when it comes to money? Not being on the same page can be a big issue in some households. It is really important that you both come from a consistent viewpoint so that your children are not getting mixed messages from you about money.

Take the time to connect, then discuss and really understand each other's points of view and ways of handling money. Look at each other's adopted roles and your family's rules, share each other's knowledge. If either or both of you are not confident with money, commit to working together to gather the information and tools you need. Read this book together.

If you are in a broken relationship, and share custody of your children, you may be facing different challenges. If you are able to communicate well with your ex-partner, put teaching the children about money in a consistent way on the agenda and share any resources you have. If communication is strained, you can take the lead, put forward your point of view, and make it your role to teach the children to have a healthy way to manage money.

Why is this relevant to teaching children about money?

Firstly, presenting a consistent and united front on the subject of money shows children a way to make money work for the family, rather than against it, and that good money management is a normal part of a loving relationship.

Secondly, without going 'over the top', there are costs to be born in the pursuit of friendship and love. It makes sense to allocate some of your budget towards this aim and to teach your children to do the same.

Teaching Children about *Connecting* with People

1. Help them to **understand that money doesn't buy love** - love comes from within them. It comes first from a healthy love and appreciation of them self. A need to buy expensive gifts for those we love is a status need, not a connecting with people need, so allocate the money for this in the appropriate 'money bag' (i.e. 'Big Toys').

There are plenty of ways to demonstrate our connection with others without over-spending - a hand-made card or gift is often appreciated so much more than a purchased card or gift.

2. Encourage your children from an early age to put some money aside in their People 'bag' so that they can **buy presents for those they love** or otherwise afford to go to the **connecting occasions** that come up - birthdays, religious celebrations, outings with friends etc. As they get older, they could save some of their People money for the larger expenses of dating, marriage (if they so choose) and setting up house with a partner.

3. Here are some suggestions to **save money whilst still connecting**:

- "Bring a plate" parties - instead of catering for parties yourself, invite your guests to bring a plate to share.
- Exercise together - as a family, or with friends.
- When considering gifts, rather than waste money on a gift that won't be appreciated, ask your child what they know about their friend or family member, and what they think that person would really like to receive.

4. Encourage your children to **decorate their People 'bag' with pictures of the important, beloved people in their lives**, and draw a diagram of where this money goes (e.g. their savings account until needed).

Action Plan:
Write down the tips from this section you plan to implement with your own family. Add any additional ideas that come to mind. Make a note of who is responsible for each item, and when it will be actioned.

Anyone who stops learning is old, whether at twenty or eighty. Anyone who keeps learning stays young. The greatest thing in life is to keep your mind young. Henry Ford

5. Learning

We each need to **learn and gather feedback**. We love to have all information to hand so that we can monitor our progress though life. We are constantly seeking and adapting to information that comes mainly through our eyes into the brain's visual processing centres. A large part of our brain is involved in processing visual cues. We use the information to monitor and regulate ourselves, adapting and learning new information that serves us along the way.

When we find a deficit in what we need to know in order to progress in a certain area of our lives, we actively seek to build our capability in that area with new information. You would not be reading this book unless you felt you had a deficit of capability in the area of teaching your children about money.

But before we teach our children, it's useful to ensure you have to hand all of the information you need. The majority of books and resources available on the subject of money play in this space of giving you information, so I'm not going to overload you with too much here. I prefer to share with you some key concepts so you can check in that you have the basics before you launch off and attempt to share potentially complex information with your children. I will also point you in the direction of resources you can use to further build your knowledge of specific areas of money management.

The first place to start is to know your own money situation. Money can be perceived as a difficult subject, and often in households it is put in the too hard basket. There's no need for this, and I enjoy showing people that it can be simple to organize what you know about money and how you handle it.

It is crucial to begin with the actual data, and to update this regularly so that you can see how well you are going. Money is a moving target and pinning it down can be problematic without a good system to organise the data.

Robert Kiyosaki and Sharon Lechter introduced me to the concept of the Financial Report Card in their book 'Rich Dad Poor Dad'. It is a simple way to present your financial data and when regularly updated, helps your brain satisfy its need to monitor your financial progress. It forms the basis of Kiyosaki's education programs, and is used in the famous 'Cashflow 101' game. Here's what a Financial Report Card can look like, and you can download one from our website (www.kidsmoneyrules.com) for your own use as often as you like.

Money Bags Financial Scorecard

Income Statement	
Income	
Import from Money Bags cashflow	
Expenses	
Import from total of each need category from Money Bags cashflow	
Monthly cash flow (Income - Expenses)	$

Balance Sheet	
Assets	**Liabilities**
Net assets (Assets - Liabilities)	$

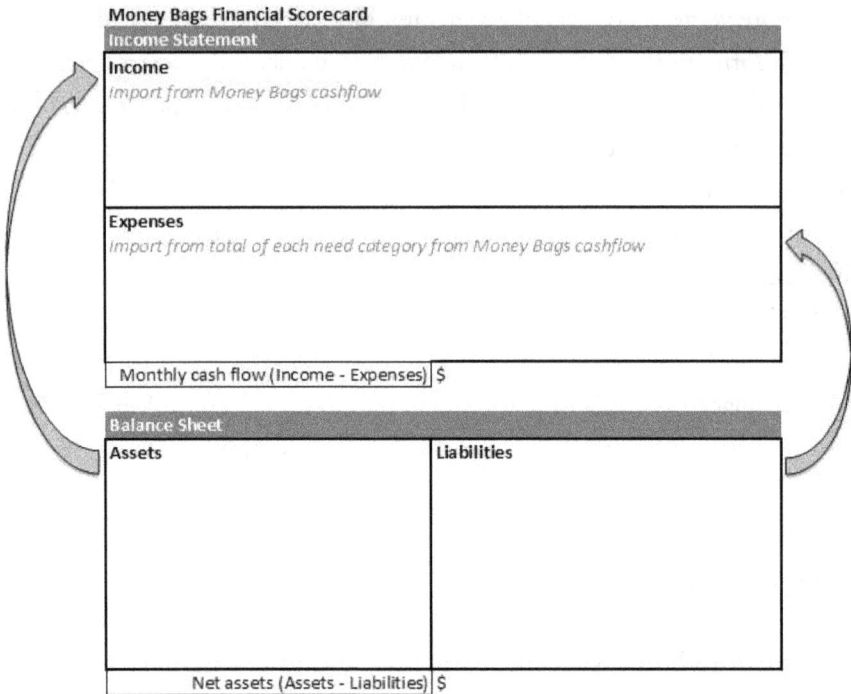

Your Financial Report Card in Three Steps

The key definitions are:

- **Income** – money that goes into your bank account – can be earned from your job or passively (i.e. cashflow earned from your assets). You win the game of money when your passive income is more than your expenses.
- **Expenses** – money that comes out of your bank account.
- **Assets** – investments that put money (passive income) into your bank account such as interest bearing deposits, bonds, rental property and stocks/shares.
- **Liabilities** – loans, debts and anything that takes money out of your bank account in the form of capital and interest repayments or costs (this definition can extend to things you and the bank may view as assets like your home or car as it costs you money to maintain these assets and they don't pay you passive income).

Whether you realize it or not, your household has a Financial Report Card. You may put it together often, or only when the bank manager asks for it so you can borrow more money. When was the last time you had a good look at your numbers?

How well are you doing in your own game of money? Can you put your own numbers on a Financial Report Card? How's that asset column coming along? Are you feeling in or out of control?

The key to gaining control of your money is to start at the point where you actually have some power – where the actual spending decisions occur. *All it takes is 3 steps:*

STEP 1

Complete a list of all the things you spend money on. If you can't list this easily (like most of us), start with your credit card and bank statements for regular expenses, and keep a spending diary for a week or so to get a handle on your incidental spending. It needn't be complex – just a piece of paper you carry with you (or even on your phone) to record how much comes out of your purse or wallet and what you spend it on as it happens or at the end of each day. If your friends are willing, ask them to help you by setting up a daily text message to report to each other your spending.

There are plenty of websites and apps with money tracking resources that you can access to help you in these tasks, and we have compiled some easy tools for you to use on our site www.kidsmoneyrules.com.

STEP 2

Have a good look at your spending in 2 ways:

1. How much is spent on the *past, present* and *future*?

2. How much is spent on each of the 6 essential needs? How does the amount you spend as a percentage of your income on each of the 6 needs compare with the commonly recommended allocation:

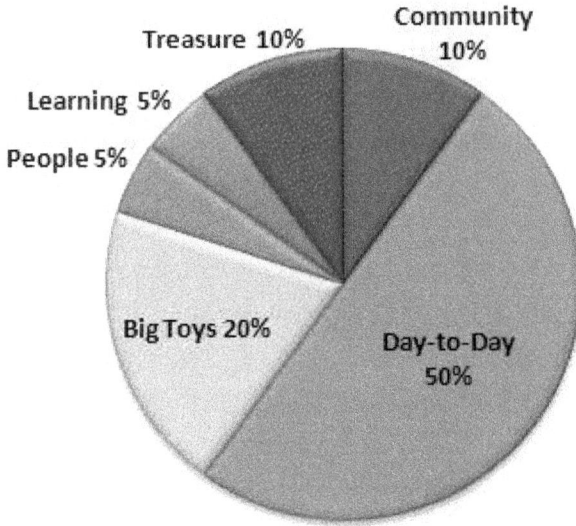

Remember to **suspend judgment when looking at your spending** – this is simply about the data, not how you feel about it. If you find yourself judging, or reacting emotionally during this exercise, jot down what you are feeling before moving on. Naming the emotion should be enough to settle it so that you can free up your brain to concentrate on the task at hand rationally. You may even find some of those less than useful scripts that have been causing resistance to financial success up until now. Jot them down so that you can replace them with new scripts allowing prosperity.

STEP 3

Decide what you want to change. Make a plan to stop or reduce spending in areas that are not helping you fulfil your own 6 essential needs, and increase spending in areas that are. This includes reducing your expenditure on the past as quickly as you can and increasing what you can spend in the present and future. Another name for this plan is a budget.

Again there are plenty of resources available to help you make your plan, and we have a cash flow spreadsheet based on the 6 Essential Needs on our website www.kidsmoneyrules.com.

If you are struggling with debt, you will need to take steps to get this under control first. Here's an approach that works for most people:

Write down on a sheet of paper, or enter into a spreadsheet each of the loans you currently owe in the following format:

Loan with	Loan for	Amount owing	Interest rate pa	Min payment
E.g. ABC Bank	Credit card	$5,000	18%	$75 per month
E.g. XYZ Finance Company	Motorbike	$20,000	5%	$470 per month
E.g. EZI Store Card	Furniture	$1,500	25%	$32 per month
Total repayments				$577 per month

In the above scenario, the repayments due total $577 per month.

Now what is the amount allocated to *Big Toys* per month i.e. savings per month + current loan repayments (including extra regular repayments) e.g. $600. $_____ per month.

If there is $600 per month allocated to big toys and the repayments total $577 per month, this leaves an excess of $23 per month.

By repaying only the minimum each month on the credit and store cards, all that is paid is the interest – the debt will never be repaid at this rate! Here's where the excess of $23 per month comes in.

Choose the smallest debt first - in this case it is the store card debt. Apply the $23 per month as an extra repayment until this debt is paid out in full, and continue to pay the other two debt repayments as usual. The repayment on the store card becomes $55 per month (was $32). Repaying at this higher rate means that this debt will be paid out completely in just over 3 years, and you have an *extra $55 per month*.

Now that the store card debt is repaid, choose the next smallest debt – in this case, the credit card. Apply the $55 as an extra payment on the credit card (i.e. the repayment becomes $130 per month). The credit card will be repaid in full in just under 5 years.

In the meantime, the motorbike has already been paid out in just under 4 years, as the $470 repayment included capital and interest.

This means that in this scenario, the debts could be fully repaid in around 8 years, **freeing up $600 per month for saving towards big toys.**

But, debt free status could be achieved even faster (*can you see how?*)

The motorbike loan was fully repaid by the end of year 4, but the credit card debt was still being repaid at $130 per month and had a further 4 years to run. By applying the full $600 per month to the credit card debt, when the motorbike loan was paid out, the repayment time on the credit card would be reduced to just 8 months. This means that **debt free status could be achieved in less than 5 years!**

Now - there are a few assumptions made in the example above:

- No further debt is incurred. The credit cards and store cards need to be destroyed if you can't resist the temptation to use them unwisely.
- Interest rates and repayment terms remain constant. Unfortunately, rates and rules do change, sometimes with

disastrous results. All the more reason to limit how much you are beholden to banks and finance companies.

- You are able to pay more than the minimum or specified payment each month. Most loans allow this these days, but check with your lender if you are not sure.

If you can't see a way to make this method work for you, seek help from a reputable qualified debt counselor (most churches and community groups can put you in touch with one).

If you are simply looking for some tools, check on the internet – most banks and financial institutions have great resources available, and we have some on our website too at www.kidsmoneyrules.com.

Now remember that money is a moving target and your brain will want to complete this exercise on a regular basis.

Part of having the data to hand so your brain can monitor progress is to have a good system to organise your money information – a filing system. Simple is best when it comes to filing, and why not use your brain's 6 essential needs as the basis of your system:

Have a file set up on your computer, and in physical form (like manila folders in a filing drawer, or a portable file) for each of the 6 essential needs:

- **Community** - here you can keep paperwork or files that pertain to your donations to community causes (you will want to keep these if you can claim a tax deduction).
- **Fun** – or *satisfying emotions* – here is where you keep information that pertains to *most day to day expenditure*. Most of this will be on your bank and credit card statements or in your spending diary (you may need your bank statements for tax, and you may want to keep receipts for warranty or insurance claims, but most of this

data you will want to keep only until you have analysed it as in step 2 above).

- **Big Toys** - or *achievements* – here is where you file information pertaining to expenditure on the big things you buy – your home, car, boat, caravan, travel etc (you will want to keep receipts, insurance certificates, warranty information, instruction manuals, maintenance journals, loan documents etc for as long as you own the item).

- **People** - or *connection* – here is where you keep information about items you buy for people you are connected to (you will want to keep valuations and insurance certificates for important jewellery like wedding, engagement and eternity rings, and you may want to keep receipts for gifts you buy for others that may need to be returned for some reason).

- **Learning** - here you keep the information you compile to keep track of your money, as well as documents that pertain to expenditure on education, training and learning (you will want to keep your tracking information so that you can check progress from time to time, and you will want your education information in case you can claim a tax deduction).

- **Treasure** – here is where you file all of the information you need to keep track of your *investments* and the measures you take to protect them (you will want to keep valuations, reports, financial plans, wills, life insurance policies etc for tax purposes, for financial planning purposes, and eventually to claim the passive income generated).

I mentioned under Learning files, documents that pertain to expenditure on education, training and learning. Most of this chapter has been devoted to teaching some basics of managing money, but you will also spend money in this category when you or family members are engaged in education of any sort.

When you have a handle on where your money is going and a plan for where you would prefer it to go, you may realize that it is important that you allocate sufficient money to the future. This is so that at some point in time, you will have the choice of whether or not you want to work for your money (the magical point in time when the passive income earned from your assets exceeds your expenditure and you have won the game of money).

I'll devote more to this topic in the next chapter about *treasure*, but as we are in learning the basics mode here, I want to give you the basics of investing in this chapter:

INVESTING BASIC 1

There are only four asset types you can invest in:

1. Cash
2. Fixed interest
3. Property
4. Stocks (Shares)

The first two of these (cash and fixed interest) are known as defensive assets, and the other two (property and stocks) are known as growth assets. All other investments are simply derived from these four (e.g. futures, options, swaps, exchange traded funds, collateralized debt obligations to name a few).

Defensive assets and growth assets behave differently, have different risks associated with them, and suit different timeframes. Risk is inherent in every investment. Most of us define risk in terms of potential to lose capital, but other important factors are potential loss of purchasing power, inability to generate the return needed to meet an investor's needs, likelihood of government rule changes, amongst others. As a rule of thumb, defensive assets carry less risk in the short term, but more in the long term, whilst growth assets carry more risk in the short term and less in the long term.

The name of the game with investing is maximizing passive income when you need it. Defensive assets are better suited if you need the passive income in the short term, and growth assets are better suited if you are accumulating assets for income in the long term. This is because good growth assets accumulate in value as the value of the income generated by them increases (helping to guard against inflation risk).

Consider a property that is rented out. If the property is well managed and maintained it will generate rental income for as long as it is tenanted. Rental agreements enable the landlord to increase the rent based on market rental returns at specified points of time. As rental returns tend to increase over the long term, so too will the value of the property.

A similar thing happens with stocks. A stock is a portion of a company that entitles the shareholder to participate in a share of its business profits (among other things). Most companies tend to pay part of their profits out to shareholders in the form of dividends. If the company is well managed, it will grow its profits over time, and depending on its dividend policy will share the growth in the form of increased dividends. As the company grows, so too does its value, the amount paid out as dividends, and the value of the shareholders' shares.

Each investor has a different tolerance for risk. It is important to understand the risk associated with each of your investments and to match your investments to your risk tolerance and time frames. A good financial advisor/planner will help you learn this for yourself and help you to make the appropriate decisions for your own investments.

INVESTING BASIC 2

Another important element to know about when investing is tax structures. These vary from country to country but most governments create incentives through tax policy to encourage their citizens to invest for their long term security. In Australia, the Superannuation Fund is a specific tax structure with tax advantages built in to reward long term investment. The ultimate reward of this structure is tax free income in retirement. The trade off for this reward is rules that limit access to your funds until retirement age or earlier death or disablement. In the USA, there are 401k Plans and in the UK, Pension Plans. There are other tax structures available to suit other investment or asset protection aims. A good financial planner will be across these and refer you to the appropriate professionals that can set them up for you.

INVESTING BASIC 3

Until you have built up enough of an asset base that the income earned from it replaces the income you earn from your work, you need insurance. You need to consider income protection, life insurance, and total and permanent disablement insurance as a minimum. As a general rule of thumb, as your asset base grows, the amount of insurance you need decreases.

Consider the following diagram:

Insurance

Net

Assets

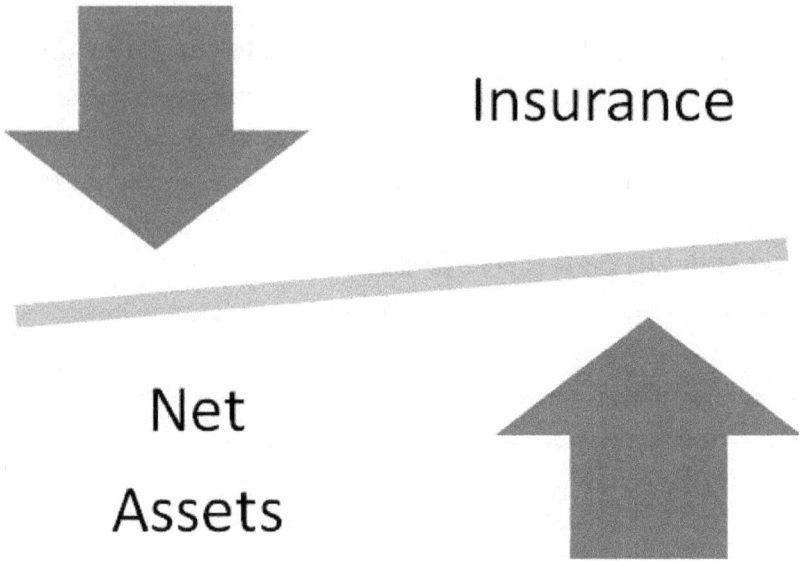

Seek help from a good financial planner or insurance adviser to set up the right plan for you and your family.

How Is This Relevant To Teaching Children About Money?

The topic of money can be very complex for an adult, let alone a child, so let's look at it from a child's point of view.

Initially, children just need to know about physically handling money. This involves learning to recognize coins and notes; and to solve simple math problems involving money like how much is something to buy, comparing value of desired items, working out how much to save, determining how much change to collect in a transaction.

As their math skills evolve, they can progress to more complex problems and the interaction of money and society. They can also handle more abstract concepts and presentation of money issues, like learning to read bank statements, tracking their bank transactions, running a small project like a party on a budget, learning about investing, running a small business.

Learning how to manage money records can start early with the Money Bags system. It is not necessary to allocate to all 6 money bags with very young children. In fact, this system has been devised to grow with them as their brain and psychology develops. Development of the 6 essential needs can be mapped to various childhood developmental models including Piaget's, Erikson's and Berne's and roughly corresponds to the following ages:

> Womb to 12 months - Community
> 6 months to 24 months - Fun
> From age 2 - Big Toys
> From age 7 - People
> From age 12 - Learning
> Late adolescence - Treasure

Each child will develop at their own pace, and for some, the traits associated with later stages of development (e.g. empathy for others, organization or learning skills, a concept of the long term) may be evident from a very young age. You will also see times where the emergence of one stage is very evident and the previous development stages seem all but forgotten. You know your own child best.

By the time a child demonstrates an interest in money (from as early as age 3), they can start learning to allocate to *Community*, *Fun* and *Big Toys*.

As the invitations start coming in from their friends to join them at birthday parties (around age 5), they can start allocating to *People* as well.

When it comes to allocating towards *Learning* and *Treasure*, it will depend on your child's concept of the future and how far that future extends. Some children will grasp the concepts at a basic level from an early age (e.g. when I finish school, I'm going to university to be a doctor, or Treasure is for when I'm a grown up), and so it will be easy and appropriate to introduce these Money Bags from the start. It is normal for a child's concept of future time to grow longer as they grow older. You will get a feel for this with Big Toys and how long they are prepared to save for. You can use the Big Toys concepts and Money Bag to gradually tease out their sense of future before introducing the Learning and Treasure Money Bags if this better suits your child.

Neuroscientists are still developing databases and studies to add to the largely observational work that has been done in the past to map human development. Some of the more interesting insights point to the development of the brain continuing well into the 20's. This has implications when defining the age at which legal adulthood begins, and helps explain why many young adults seem to have no concept of the future and live just for today.

In addition, the discovery of Neuroplasticity shows the brain's ability to continue changing and re-learning throughout adulthood.

There is no right or wrong way to work with the Money Bags, except to ensure your children learn to allocate the money they earn to each of the 6 essential needs. If these are covered off by the time they reach their late teens/early adulthood, you will have done a great job of setting them up for a life of financial success.

Teaching Children to Value Learning

Valuing lifelong learning, and being able to organize and use information are attributes that set successful people apart. Teaching children to value their education is vitally important.

1. **Talk about the cost of education** as your children progress through school. Even their early education.

2. Prepare them to contribute to this cost when they are able to work. Studies show that **children who worked through Uni or College place a much higher value on their education** than those whose parents paid their way. Learning to apply for grants and scholarships also sets children up for success in their working lives.

3. Teach them that **learning doesn't stop when they leave school** or tertiary education. There will always be something new to learn and lots of ways to learn. Be an example of this by letting them know that you are reading this book to learn new things to make their life better.

4. Show your children how to **set up a basic filing system for their money related documents** as part of them learning to keep their belongings organized. Use the name of each Money Bag as the file category (i.e. a file each for Community, Fun, Big Toys, People, Learning, and Treasure). You'll be able to access a template of these when you join up at www.kidsmoneyrules.com.

5. **Make learning about money fun** with some of the teaching aids you can download from our website www.kidsmoneyrules.com when you join.

6. Have them **decorate their Learning 'bag'** with pictures of things they are interested in learning, or schools they would like to get into when older. Add a diagram of where this money goes (i.e. into their savings account until needed).

Action Plan:
Write down the tips from this section you plan to implement with your own family. Add any additional ideas that come to mind. Make a note of who is responsible for each item, and when it will be actioned.

Treasure

A big part of financial freedom is having your heart and mind free from worry about the what-ifs of life. Suze Orman

6. Treasure

Each of us love moving forward based on hope for the future. Anticipating a positive future provides impetus for us to move forward. In fact, when we are unable to see a positive future, we 'freeze', or get stuck. Happily, in nature, the default position of the world is positive – consider how quickly a forest regrows after a fire or destructive storm, or how a plant can establish itself in a crack in concrete. The human tendency to look forward, and to aim for constant improvement was referred to by the ancient Greeks as 'physis'. It is inbuilt in each of us to grasp for any sign of a positive future even after the most devastating of events in our lives.

Some of us are better at envisioning our future than others, even though we each have the innate ability to anticipate. Some of us are more expansive in our vision than others and are able to anticipate and plan for more in our lives. The good news is that as we each have this ability, we can develop it if even if up until now it has been under-utilised.

A great way to look forward is to construct a vision board. When anticipating the point in time in the future when you no longer need to work for your income, you will want to include all of the essential things your brain needs to have a full life i.e. Community, Fun, Big Toys, People, Learning and Treasure.

If you are not confident that you have considered all you need for the future, try constructing a vision board that includes a picture or representation of what you want in each of these essential categories.

Having a positive future is one thing, funding it is another. You will need income throughout your lifetime, and there will come a time when you either can't, or no longer wish to, work for it. This is the time when you will rely on the treasures in your treasure chest to see you through.

In your treasure chest you should have:

- Something to provide cash in case of the unexpected – at least 3 months of net income at easy reach - and insurance policies to replace big toys, pay medical expenses, or provide short term replacement of income in case of disaster.
- Something to provide passive income that at least covers your family's debts, planned major expenditure and living expenses. These are your assets and can include cash, fixed interest, property and shares depending on your timeframe and risk tolerance, as well as insurance policies to replace capital that you are not able to accumulate if you or your partner die or become permanently disabled.
- Structure and documentation aimed at protecting your assets, and providing the optimum tax treatment for your capital and income. These can include trust deeds, company or partnership documentation, wills, death benefit nominations, insurance policies.

The earlier you start the better, but it is never too late to make a difference to your future money outcomes.

A good financial planner will work with you to determine how much passive income you will need when you want to be in a position to choose to work or not, and how to accumulate and protect your treasure chest.

How is this relevant to teaching children about money?

Whilst most children live in the moment, they are also able to use their imagination to create amazing things. Harness this imagination early to get them thinking ahead to what an ideal life might be like for them as adults.

Children have the huge advantage of time on their side. An early start to their treasure chest will mean that they will not have to allocate as much throughout their adult lives. As soon as they can grasp it, explain the concept of compound interest to them, and the advantage of starting early. For example:

> $1,000 invested at age 10 earning just 3% after tax will grow to over $5,000 by age 65.
> If it was invested instead at age 20, it would grow to only $3,781 by age 65.
> If you left it until age 30 to invest it, the result would be just $2,814.

You can explain that higher returns should result in more treasure, but come with higher risk (mainly in the short term as I explained in the previous chapter). Using our previous example:

$1,000 invested at age 10 earning 6% after tax will grow to almost $25,000 by age 65.

If it was invested instead at age 20, it would grow to $13,765 by age 65. If you left it until age 30 to invest it, the result would be $7,686.

This is a simple but important concept to teach to your children who will have so much more time working on their side than we adults have.

Teaching Children about their Treasure

1. Children love doing vision boards - **encourage them to construct their vision boards** and stretch how far forward they see. Ask them to include at least one thing they might want to have in their imagined adult lives from each of the 6 essential needs. Talk about what these might be:

- Community - will they want to continue supporting their current community projects?
- Fun - will they want to continue having the day to day life they lead now including a nice home, good food, clean water, toys, entertainment?
- Big Toys - what are some big toys they might buy - a car, travels, nice clothes, jewelry, art?
- People - who are the special people they will want to spend time with? Do they think they'll get married, have children, live close to or far from family?
- Learning - will they want to go to University, follow a special interest, learn new things?
- Treasure - will they always want to have something to fall back on?

2. The best advice you can give children is to **start investing early and make it as easy as possible** by investing a small amount on a regular basis now and throughout their working lives. You could act as the paymaster and deduct the amount allocated to treasure and invest it for them until they start working. As soon as they get a job, they should arrange with their paymaster to deduct their treasure amount and transfer it to a separate bank account set up only for investment.

3. **Your children need two bank accounts** - one is for transactions - Community, Fun, Big Toys, People and Learning. These are for short to medium term spending so access to the money is more important than interest earned.

The second account is a higher interest earning account (e.g. online savings account) where they put their treasure money. This money will **never be spent**. Instead it will be invested. I recommend at least 10% of their allowance be allocated to this account.

4. **Investing in growth assets** can start with as little as $1,000 in their Treasure account. A good financial planner will help you set up appropriate investments for your children.

5. Encourage them to decorate their Treasure 'bag' with pictures from their vision boards, and draw a diagram of where this money goes (i.e. it goes to their higher interest earning investment account, for long term investing).

Action Plan:
Write down the tips from this section you plan to implement with your own family. Add any additional ideas that come to mind. Make a note of who is responsible for each item, and when it will be actioned.

"Money was never a big motivation for me, except as a way to keep score. The real excitement is playing the game." Donald Trump

Part 4 - Where is Our World Heading?

Some Final Thoughts:
Where is our world heading?
And how do you play your part?

Setting ourselves and our children up for success, freedom and power with money is more important now than it has ever been. Our world is changing rapidly. There is a growing gap between those that have, and those that have not. And I don't just mean money. I'm talking about choices, I'm talking about being in control of what's happening rather than having circumstances control you, I'm talking about having freedom, power and success in all areas of your life.

Those of us who don't make the choice to be the drivers of our own lives will be left behind. From a brain science point of view, it will be those that allow their system 1 limbic brains to be in control most of the time. From a personal development point of view, it will be those who choose not to work on their internal world. From a spiritual point of view, it will be those who choose not to draw closer to the divine by learning who they really are and the unique gifts they bring to the world.

How do you get into the driver's seat of your life? It's counter-intuitive at first, because you need to learn to let go of some things rather than tighten control. Find the patterns of habitual behavior that are no longer serving you and let them go. Take the time to really get to know yourself and how you would prefer to satisfy your basic needs from a place of love – love for yourself, your community, and all of humanity.

Thankfully, there is now a movement in the world towards greater cooperation and love – have you noticed it?

You don't have to do this on your own – there are plenty of people and resources to help you.

The place to start is in your own home, and with your own children.

We have the opportunity right here, right now, to create a sustainable future for ourselves, and for the planet. Play your part.

Finally, use your family's money mindfully. Teach your children to do the same by:

- having them handle actual cash BEFORE more abstract versions of money,
- requiring them to earn their money, and
- showing them how to allocate their money towards living a full and significant life.

And a full and significant life is exactly what I wish for you and your family!

Now … go and teach your children what the truly rich teach their children to be happy and manage money with ease.

For resources and further information please sign up to our website at www.kidsmoneyrules.com. And … while you are at it, I'd love some feedback (or a review on Amazon) about what you like most and least about this book so that I can make it better.

Appendix A

We have seen record levels of **personal debt** in Western economies

In the United States (2012)

"U.S. household consumer debt profile:

- Average credit card debt: $15,257
- Average mortgage debt: $149,782
- Average student loan debt: $34,703

In total, American consumers owe:

- $11.31 trillion in debt - a decrease of 0.7% from last year
- $849 billion in credit card debt
- $8.03 trillion in mortgages
- $956 billion in student loans - an increase of 4.6% from last year" (10)

Outstanding Consumer Credit in the US stood at over $2,778 billion dollars at the end of 2012. (11)

In the United Kingdom (2012)

In the UK "outstanding personal debt stood at £1.457 trillion at the end of February 2012.

- This is up from £1.452 trillion at the end of February 2011.

- Individuals owed nearly as much as the entire country produced during the whole of 2011." (12)

In Australia (2010)

According to Veda (provider of credit information and analysis in Australia and New Zealand):

"Veda's bi-annual Australian Debt Study released today, reveals a growing number of Australian consumers are feeling the pressure, with 82 per cent admitting they are worried about meeting future debt repayments, up from 75 per cent in September 2010.

The results also show just over half (55%) of Australians are comfortable that their current level of debt is within their budget, down from 62 per cent in 2010 - the lowest ever recorded result since the survey began in 2007.

One in five Australians surveyed admit they are struggling to repay their current credit commitments, whilst more than a third (35%) have received assistance from family or friends to repay debts and a quarter have sold assets." (13)

"According to the HILDA Survey*, average debt per household increased by 5 per cent per annum in real terms between 2006 and 2010…)." (14) * Household, Income and Labour Survey in Australia.

Children are tending to 'leave the nest' at older ages

It seems we are tending to raise dependant teenagers and young adults that haven't been taught how to look after themselves. Many become what are known as *boomerang children*.

In Australia the average age to leave home is 25. (15)

In the US, according to Census Bureau figures, almost half of adult children between 18 and 24 live with their parents (56 percent of men and 43 percent of women).

Children are leaving home in their late teens/early adulthood, then returning when they find it too hard to manage in the 'real' world. Consider this quote from a popular online magazine for seniors lamenting the effect this phenomena is having on retirement dreams:

"There are reasons why birds kick their youngsters out of the nest and make them fly. It's because the baby birds are too afraid to do it on their own, and if the baby isn't kicked out, it will never develop the wing strength to fly later when they are heavier. Substitute humans into this idea and the same holds true.

Of course you love your child. But that doesn't give them the right to descend on you at will, disrupt your household, and make life miserable.

You wouldn't take that from another adult, so don't do your adult child the disservice of letting them get away with it.

What's more, it zaps your personal power over your own life and your own home. You give him your personal power, it does him no good, and both of you are left with nothing." (16)

There are some serious implications for our children if we don't teach them to 'fly' in the real world – for example, not ever owning their own home:

"This study has uncovered a positive association between the age at which young adults leave the family home and the likelihood of them becoming homeowners in their 30s. However, this finding is true only until a person reaches their mid-

20s. Beyond about age 25, the later their departure, the lower their probability of being a homeowner themselves in their 30s.

Furthermore, it seems that boomerang children who return to live with their parents after initially leaving, are less likely to be homeowners in their 30s than those who left the family home only once. This is especially the case among persons who came back to live with their parents because they lost their jobs or were having financial problems." (17)

About the Author

Leanda Kayess Dip FP (1960-) was born in Sydney, Australia, grew up and married in Sydney before moving to Cairns, Far North Queensland, Australia in 1994. For thirty years she worked in the financial world, the last 11 of these advising clients as a Certified Financial Planner. Her first book, "Money Bags: What Rich Parents Teach Their Kids To Be Happy And Avoid Debt", is an extract from her larger work "How To Talk Money With Kids". Her books combine her financial expertise with her passion for and lifetime study of human potential, bringing a fresh 'people friendly' approach to the subject of money based on the way our brains and systems function.

Bibliography and References

[1] NeuroPower Learning and Development. www.learnneuropower.com

[2] Harv. T. Ecker 'Secrets of the Millionaire Mind: Mastering the Inner Game of Wealth' Harper Business 2005

[3] Doidge N, MD 'The Brain That Changes Itself' Scribe Publications 2009, p.308,309

[4] Leiberman M, Berkman 'The Neuroscience of Goal Pursuit' UCLA (2008).

[5] Eisenberger N I et al. 'An experimental study of shared sensitivity to physical pain and social rejection' Pain 126 (2006) p. 132-138

[6] Anthony J. Decasper and Melanie J. Spence. University of North Carolina at Greensboro. 'Prenatal Maternal Speech Influences Newborns' Perception of Speech Sounds*'. Infant Behavior And Development 9, 1X3-150 (1986)

[7] Charles Zeanahand Anna Smyke (Tulane University); Nathan Fox(University of Maryland; Sebastian Koga (University of Virginia); Dana Johnson (University of Minnesota); Peter Marshall (Temple University); Charles A. Nelson(Harvard Medical School); *Subproject investigators include Megan Gunnar, Jennifer Windsor

[8] Tabinia G, Lieberman M D, Ann. N.Y. Acad Sci.1118: p90-101 (2007)

[9] Putting Feelings Into Words; Affect Labeling Disrupts Amygdala Activity in Response to Affective Stimuli - Matthew D. Lieberman, Naomi I. Eisenberger, Molly J. Crockett, Sabrina M. Tom, Jennifer H. Pfeifer, and Baldwin M. Way. University of California, Los Angeles PSYCHOLOGICAL SCIENCE Volume 18

[10] Current as of February 2013 http://www.nerdwallet.com/blog/credit-card-data/average-credit-card-debt-household/

[11] Board of Governors of the Federal Reserve System Consumer Credit Update February 7, 2013

[12] National Credit Charity – Credit Action

[13] www.veda.com 2011

[14] RBA Bulletin March 2012

[15] Australian Bureau of Statistics Census 2011

[16] Senior Magazine

[17] Staying at home longer to become homeowners? Martin Turcotte an analyst in the Social and Aboriginal Statistics Division, Statistics Canada.

For resources and further information please sign up at our website www.kidsmoneyrules.com. And ... while you are at it, I'd love some feedback about what you like most and least about this book so that I can make it better. Regards Leanda Kayess Dip FP